A WORLD SERIES OF POKER CHAMPION'S
GUIDE TO MASTERING INTERNET POKER

SCOTT FISCHMAN

Book design: Christina Bliss and Mary Sexton
Cover design: Bashan Aquart, SpotCo

FIRST EDITION

10 9 8 7 6 5 4 3 2 1

CONTENTS

Foreword

WHEN SCOTT FISCHMAN AND the Crew (as ESPN nicknamed him and his colorful group of friends) burst onto the poker scene at the 2004 World Series of Poker, no one knew too much about them beyond the fact that they were young guys brimming with talent. Now, just two years later, you'd be hard-pressed to find too many people capable of recalling everyone who was a member of the Crew. Yet no one has forgotten about Scott, whose name remains well-known throughout the poker world. He has backed up his serious game with some equally serious staying power.

In 2005, he nearly pulled the impossible, finishing second in the World Series event he'd won the previous year. Let's take a closer look at this feat: The $1,500 buy-in no-limit tournament is one of the most heavily attended events on the World Series calendar. In 2004, he had to defeat a field of nearly 1,000 players. His second-place finish in 2005 came against more than 2,300 players! The whole poker world was suddenly abuzz about Scott Fischman, and rightly so—six money finishes at the WSOP, including two bracelets (the coveted prize awarded to winners of WSOP events), in just two years is nothing to sneeze at!

Scott kept the buzz going throughout the year with his renowned Internet poker exploits. Along the way, I handpicked him for my Camp Hellmuth poker fantasy camp staff, and he didn't let me down. His lucid, penetrating explanations of how to play hands convinced me that this guy knows the game and earned him rave reviews from all the campers. Fischman doesn't only know how to play the game, he knows how to *teach* it. And his ability to communicate well (besides being one of the cornerstones of the writing of a great book like the one you're holding) puts him at the top of my list for future fantasy camps.

How did Scott acquire all that poker knowledge? Good old-fashioned hard work and practice, practice, practice. He hasn't hurt himself playing eight tables of online poker at one time—thus reaching in a matter of months a level of experience (as measured by hands played) that other pros have spent years acquiring. Armed with his laptop, Scott has torched the online poker world for tons of money and scores of tournament titles. Best of all, his nontraditional way of learning the game has allowed him to learn—and to present to you—some great nontraditional moves!

I have enjoyed watching Scott break into the poker world and gain the respect of his peers. There's only one road to respect in this world: winning money and tournaments and beating the other top players. Perhaps the most significant measure of whether a poker player has gained abiding respect is the willingness of other pros to bet on him to win. Twice now—in Monte Carlo and Las Vegas—Fischman asked me to take a piece of his action in a heads-up match. Both times I was happy to oblige, to the tune of more than $10,000 of my own money.

I've watched Scott win tournaments and win side games in both in the brick-and-mortar and online worlds. Winning in these different disciplines and environments demonstrates that he has a wealth of sound poker knowledge, knowledge he shares in this book. So arm yourself with his tactics, and I'll see you—at least those of you who take the time to master these tactics—at a final table soon!

—Phil Hellmuth, Jr., nine-time World Series of Poker champion, and author of *Play Poker Like the Pros*

Introduction

I STARTED PLAYING POKER for the same reason a lot of people do: I lost money much less quickly than I did playing other games.

When I was 18, I went to visit a high school friend attending college in Arizona, a state where, at the time, anyway, 18-year-olds could legally gamble. We ended up spending most of our time in a casino on an Indian reservation, and I returned home with a new hobby.

I suppose I should mention that home was Las Vegas, where I was gainfully employed as a valet parking attendant at a well-known hotel-casino. It was a brutal job—pretty much a sprint from start to finish in a polyester suit under the scorching desert sun—but the customers tipped, and they tipped well. The end of each workday meant two things: I'd be exhausted, and I'd have $200 cash burning a hole in my pocket.

The legal age to gamble in Vegas is 21, but a fake ID wasn't hard to come by. I played blackjack, craps, roulette, you name it. Sometimes I won big. More often, I lost. But it never mattered—another day of parking cars, and my bankroll would soon be replenished.

As I said, I gravitated toward poker because the bleeding was slower. You can lose $100 in a second at blackjack. It takes a lot longer to lose the same amount at a $3/$6 Hold'em table, even if you're trying. Poker tournaments turned out to be an even better value—for a small entry fee, I could gamble for hours.

When I finally turned 21, I was old enough to gamble legally and, more important, get a job inside a casino, away from that merciless sun. A friend told me the Orleans needed temporary dealers for a monthlong series of poker tournaments. It wasn't hard getting hired. Poker tournaments are where the cardrooms break in their inexperienced dealers, as they don't have to do much besides deliver the cards and monitor the betting.

My career as a tournament dealer lasted less than a day. When my new bosses saw that I could actually shuffle and pitch with a reasonable amount of dexterity, they pulled me out of the tournaments and put me to work in the real money games.

Imagine, on your first day as a waiter, getting thrown into the kitchen and asked to prepare eight meals at once. A dealer in a cash game has to be able to calculate and remove the correct rake—the cut for the house—on every hand. Dealers are constantly rotated from table to table and must be able to switch, say, from $2/$4 Hold'em to $20/$40 seven-card stud hi-lo to pot-limit Omaha without missing a beat. And it's not enough just to be accurate. A cash-game dealer has got to be fast. Faster dealing means more hands, and more hands means more rakes for the house, not to mention more tips for the dealer.

I'd been thrown to the wolves, but I quickly discovered I loved the company. I soaked up every bit of information that I could while dealing and practiced in my spare time. Soon enough, I found another job dealing at the Sahara. Not the most glamorous room in town, but a good place to learn and perfect my skills. Eventually I moved up to the Mirage, still one of the best cardrooms in Vegas.

When my shifts ended, I simply moved to the other side of the table. Before too long, I was playing $20/$40 and $30/$60 Hold'em and whatever nightly tournaments I could find. I wasn't a great player, but I was learning to hold my own.

My body, however, was wearing out. I developed rheumatoid arthritis, which at times got so painful that I couldn't walk, let alone deal. A year and a half after earning my job at the Mirage, I was forced to retire.

I'm a big believer in the idea that things happen for a reason. While playing a series of tournaments in Reno, I met a group of crazy Canadian poker players. Every night, after they finished playing in the tournaments, they'd return to their rooms and play online. They turned out to be "prop" players, employed by one of the big virtual cardrooms to keep certain games alive. With some help from my new friends from the north, I was soon working a regular shift playing online $3/$6 stud.

Unlike props in real brick-and-mortar cardrooms—who generally get paid hourly—online props typically get paid by the hand. It didn't take long for me to figure out that the way to really make money online was to see more hands. I began "multi-tabling," often playing four (or more) games at the same time.

Now here's where I make a confession: I have never read a poker book. I have nothing against them; I've just never been much of a reader. Everything I know about poker I've learned at the table, or in discussions about hands away from the table.

Later, I would meet the great Doyle Brunson, who would tell me that this was the same way he learned to play. He spent hours at the poker table, followed by hours in his room, where he and his friends would deal themselves hand after hand, trying to figure out which strategies worked best in specific situations, slowly developing an intuitive sense of the odds. To put this knowledge into action, Doyle used to drive thousands of miles a year in search of games, testing what he'd learned and experimenting with new strategies.

I got better at poker in much the same way, except that I had online poker. It didn't just speed up the learning curve, it demolished it. In live cardrooms, I had been able to play about 40 hands an hour. Multi-tabling online, often across multiple sites, I could see 400 hands an hour. My game took off. Doyle won his first World Series bracelet at age 42. I earned two—thanks to online poker—before my 25th birthday.

The Internet has radically transformed the process of learning poker. Anybody with a computer and enough dedication can play thousands of hands a day, spotting patterns, discovering familiar situations. A novice can become a seasoned veteran in a matter of weeks. The length of time it takes to become a great player can now be measured in months instead of years.

It doesn't matter where you live, what time it is, or even how much money you have—you can always find a game that will suit your needs. With dedication, observation, and discipline, the Internet can help you become a champion. Without having to read a book.

So at this point you're probably wondering two things: 1) why a guy who has never read a book on poker decided to write one, and 2) why you should bother reading it.

Fair enough. The truth is, while I've never read a book to improve my play, I certainly have had a lot of help. It would have been impossible for me to enjoy as much success as quickly as I have without a lot of input from my friends. I have been lucky enough to receive tons of advice on which games to play and how to play them. I've spent countless hours with great players, breaking down their strategies and incorporating them into my own style of play.

You're not going to find an odds percentage chart in this book or any theories on, say, when to check-raise an opponent on the turn. There aren't any equations to memorize or math problems for you to solve.

Contrary to popular belief, there is no "right" way to play poker. There is only the opportunity to develop a style that will work for you.

What you will find are the shortcuts I've discovered that can help you become a better player faster. My goal is not to teach you how to play winning poker, but to help you learn how to learn to become a better player. I've tried to share everything I know about online poker, from making your first deposit to the "Factors" I look for in analyzing a game. You'll find some of my favorite strategies and techniques, presented not as gospel but as a starting point for you to develop your own favorite strategies and techniques. I've also included advice from several friends I believe to be the best online players in the world. While putting this book together, I e-mailed them the same question: "What is your No. 1 tip for aspiring players?" You'll find their responses throughout the book.

Basically, this is the poker book I would have read if I had ever read a book on poker. Even if you're like me—a less-than-enthusiastic reader—you can pick up plenty of information just by skimming the pages. (Just pretend you're reading CliffsNotes—I've even highlighted the critical concepts for you!)

Okay, enough small talk. Time to turn the page ...

CHAPTER ONE:
Getting Started

FIRST OF ALL, YOU probably think poker is a game you play against other people. And you're probably half right. To succeed at the game, you're going to have to spend a lot of time thinking about how other people think and how their thinking translates into action.

But the other half of the equation—maybe even more than half—is learning to understand *yourself*. Why you do the things you do. Or don't do the things you're supposed to do. To be a consistently successful player, you are going to have to remain both aggressive and optimistic during the times when nothing seems to be going right. Nearly every great poker player has an arsenal of mental tricks he uses to stay on top of his game, maintain a positive outlook, and assist with critical decisions.

> **A huge part of your poker success will come from understanding your own psychology.**

We'll get into some of the specifics later. Suffice to say for now that to play your best poker, you've got to be comfortable with both yourself and your surroundings. I'm not just talking about finding a way to relax at the final table of a World Series event when they dump a wheelbarrow full of hundred-dollar bills onto the center of the table. It all begins with the first hand you play at a $1/$2 limit table.

Choosing a Game

I'm often asked what my favorite game is. My answer is always the same: "Whatever they're dealing." I started my online career playing in seven-card stud ring games. I got on TV playing no-limit Hold'em tournaments. I earned a World Series bracelet playing H.O.R.S.E.—a tournament that alternates, from hand to hand, among Hold'em, Omaha, Razz, Seven-Card Stud, and Hi-Lo Seven Card Stud Eight-or-Better.

Despite the success I have enjoyed playing all these different games, only very recently did I become comfortable enough with my abilities to start playing high-limit cash games. What was holding me back? I figured out very early on that while I might be risking about the same amount of money in a $5,000 buy-in tournament and a $200/$400 limit game, the mind-set required to beat each of these games is totally different. It's okay, for example, to get bluffed off a hand in a no-limit tournament, where preserving your (irreplaceable) chips is of utmost importance. But the same laydown might represent a critical mistake in a cash game. It was only after a long period of careful thought about this—and all the other differences between the two styles of play—that I felt comfortable enough to start playing the big-money cash games.

What does this mean for you? I highly, highly recommend that you start with one game. You want to play Omaha hi-lo cash games? Then stay away from the multi-table no-limit Hold'em tournaments.

The differences between the two games—and the games within the games—are so great that you're more likely to wind up confused than having developed a real feel for either game.

I'm not saying you should never switch games, just that you should give each game you're interested in an "exclusive" window—a week, a month, etc.—to give yourself the best possible opportunity to learn as much as you can about what it takes to beat it.

> **Trying to learn several forms of poker at once is a good way to learn none of them well. Start with one game and stick with it long enough to gather results you can analyze.**

I happen to think that the best place for new players to start—especially those interested in going on to play major tournaments—is no-limit "Sit-N-Go" tournaments. They are widely available on nearly every site, offer a built-in stop-loss (you can only lose your entry fee), and provide immediate exposure to the benefits of shifting strategies throughout a tournament. All this in an hour. I like Sit-N-Gos so much that I've dedicated an entire chapter to them.

Know Your Limits

If you decide to start with cash, or "ring" games, you'll need to know that they come in three different varieties.

The most structured form—and the easiest to master—is *limit* poker. As the name suggests, there are limits on the amounts you can bet. In most limit games, you'll be required to bet in certain increments that begin at one level, then increase later in the hand. For example, in $2/$4 limit Hold'em, you'll bet in $2 increments before and immediately following the flop—called the small bet—then in $4 increments on the turn and river—the big bet. (If you're unfamiliar with the terms *flop*, *turn*, and *river*, you should probably read the glossary and the rules located in this book's appendices before sitting down to play.)

When I play limit poker, I like to buy in for 30 big bets. It's usually enough for me to withstand an early dry spell or a run of bad luck, but not so much that I can't make it back in a session or two if I lose it all. I don't like to rebuy in a limit game. If my chips dwindle to less than I might need to play out a full hand—say, five big bets or so—then it's probably not my day. I'll save whatever I've got left to make a fresh start tomorrow.

In no-limit poker, you are allowed to bet as much of your stack as you want at any time. This is the kind of poker you usually see on TV: When a player pushes *all-in*, he's decided to risk all of the chips he has in front of him on the outcome of the hand. The numbers in a $2/$4 no-limit game don't correspond to the amount you can bet, but rather the size of the small and big blinds posted before the flop.

There is a world of difference between a $2/$4 limit game (where a wild pot might reach $40) and a $2/$4 no-limit game (where the pots will often grow to hundreds of dollars). There's usually no hard-and-fast rule as to how much to buy in for in a no-limit game; what's important is that you have enough chips in relation to the other players at the table. An opponent with a lot more chips than you can force you to play for all your chips on every hand, which is definitely *not* a good way to feel comfortable at the table. Keep in mind also that there are a lot of strategic differences between limit and no-limit poker—some players say they're as alike as checkers and chess—and you may want to avoid switching between the two styles of play until you're sure you have a handle on one.

Pot-limit poker, by contrast, is a hybrid of the two, allowing players to bet up to the current size of the pot at any given time. It's a deceptively tricky form of poker to master, so you may want to avoid it until you've spent some time with one or both of the other styles.

How Much to Play For

Once you've chosen the type of game you're going to play, you've got to decide what kind of stakes you're willing to play for. Before I offer any advice, I'm going to give you a mantra that will set you free:

IT'S NOT ABOUT WINNING OR LOSING

Okay, Scott. What the hell are you talking about? Of course poker is about winning and losing. The good players take money from the bad ones. Don't they?

Sure they do. But as much as skill accounts for success in poker, luck still plays a huge role. The best poker players in the world suffer through losing nights, losing weeks, even losing months. In fact, they lose many more poker tournaments than they win. What these players understand, however, is that winning isn't the goal. It's a by-product of the actual goal: making good decisions at the poker table.

> **Winning is not the goal, but the by-product of making good decisions at the poker table.**

As nice as winning is, the success or failure of a poker session isn't measured by the amount of money you've won. The question you need to ask yourself at the end of each session is this: "Did I consistently put myself in a position to win as much money as I could by making correct decisions?"

This is especially important for new players. You need to look at your first few months at the poker table as a sort of probationary period. A player who loses his entire initial stake but manages to master a few of the game's critical concepts is, in the long run, going to be in a much better position than someone who makes a few quick scores while developing bad habits at the table.

We'll talk about some of those critical concepts and bad habits later. For now, we'll return to the question that started it all: how much to deposit online to begin.

When offering advice to new players, some people advocate starting with free games. There's an obvious benefit to this strategy—you'll get to see how hands play out without having to risk any actual money. But if you're serious about learning the game, you may be doing yourself a disservice.

Poker is meant to be played for money. Period. It's the way we keep score, the measurement that distinguishes a good player from a bad one.

The problem with free games is that there's no incentive to play well, or more accurately, no disincentive to playing badly. You can enter every pot and stay in each hand until the end without any concern for strategy. Regardless of whether you find this enjoyable, it's not poker. It's bingo!

The goal of every serious poker player I know is to learn something new during every single session. That's just not going to happen in a free game. You're much more likely to develop bad habits than learn good ones.

So how much should you deposit? Let's start with a moment of honesty: There is a very good chance you are going to lose your entire first deposit.

I'm not saying you're definitely going to lose. You may discover that you are a fast study with a natural gift for the game. Maybe you'll run into players who know even less than you do. You might even experience a phenomenal run of luck, tripling or quadrupling your bankroll during your very first session.

But you probably won't. You should look at your first deposit as the price of an education. Your tuition to poker school. An investment in a set of skills that, down the line, will more than pay for itself.

Before you get too discouraged by that reality check, you may want to remember that there's a huge difference between poker and school (at least for me): Poker is fun! It's going to be an educational experience, but it's also going to be entertaining.

How much should you be willing to risk on your initial deposit? How much would you spend on a dinner date? Start off with an amount you'd be willing to shell out during a date on a Friday night. If you're a Mickey D's–and–a–movie kind of person, start with $40. If you're a high roller who'd drop $300 on a fancy dinner, then start with $300.

A good rule of thumb when starting out is to avoid gambling with more than you'd spend on a dinner date—at worst, you'll pay for an hour or two of entertainment!

Remember, the point—at least at first—isn't going to be winning or losing. You're going to be studying the game, absorbing as much as you can. As I said before, poker is a game that has to be played for money, so you want the losses to sting just a little bit—but not so much that they prevent you from learning or experimenting with different styles. Lose your initial stake, write it off as a bad date. If the cards fall your way and you score big, well, I think you get the metaphor.

Choosing a Site

I chose my first online site for a simple reason: My friends played there. They told me which games I should play and the best times to play them. I didn't even have to go through the stress of making an initial deposit—I simply gave some cash to one of my friends, who transferred an equal sum into my online account.

If you've got friends who play regularly, you could do a lot worse than asking them for advice. If you don't, there's no need to worry— you're going to learn how to do it yourself.

Choosing a site is a lot like picking out a new car, except that if you're anything like me, you're going to spend a lot more time on the site than you would behind the wheel. You wouldn't buy a new car without taking it for a test-drive. You should do the same thing with an online poker room.

Before you deposit any money into an online account, spend some time "test-driving" three or four sites you might be interested in.* It's not going to cost you anything except time—the downloads are free, and nearly every site offers "play money" games that don't require you to risk a cent of real cash. (Basically, these test-drives are the only reason you should be playing free games.)

What should you be looking for? Here are some things to keep in mind:

SEE WHAT THEY'RE SPREADING

Your first stop at every site will be the lobby, the single most valuable source of information about a particular site. We'll talk more about how to analyze this information in the next chapter; for now, your focus should be on making sure the site offers the kinds of games you're looking for at the times you plan on playing. Every site has its

---

*If you don't know where to start, you might want to use popularity as your guide. Check out a site like Poker Pulse (*www.pokerpulse.com*) to see which sites are currently attracting the most players.

peaks and valleys—there might be a ton of seven-card stud action on the weekends, but almost none during your weekday lunch hour. Your progress as a multi-table tournament Hold'em stud is going to suffer if the site you're on offers only one or two tournaments a week. You get the idea.

PROMOTIONS AND FREEROLLS

With so many sites to choose from, it's definitely a buyer's market. Nearly every online cardroom offers some kind of deposit bonus—just keep in mind that you'll usually have to play a certain number of hands before you're eligible to receive the bonus money. You'll also find "freerolls," tournaments that allow you to win real money without risking any of your own. Many sites also have customer-loyalty programs, awarding points for regular play that can be traded in for merchandise or entry into real-money tournaments.

SPECIAL FEATURES

Every site is a little bit different, offering its own set of special features. Some of them (like choosing your own avatar) are mostly cosmetic, but others (such as the ability to see your opponents' hand histories) are actually incredibly useful. A lot of sites offer buddy lists, notifying you when your favorite players have logged onto the site. (Keep in mind that when I say "favorite," I'm not talking about the players you like the most, but the players you like playing with the most, if you get my drift.) Look for the little things a site offers that can help you find an edge. They add up.

LOOK AND FEEL

Take a seat at one of the tables and take a look around. You're going to be spending a lot of time interacting with this screen. If the table is a particular shade of purple that annoys you after 15 minutes, imagine how you'll feel after 15 hours. Maybe the raise and fold buttons are in a place that feels counterintuitive, you don't like the slider bar on the pot-limit Omaha table, or the sound effects grate on your nerves. You're going to experience a wide range of emotions at the poker table—even a virtual one—and it's a good idea to avoid anything that will exacerbate the negative ones.

Many sites allow you to customize your experience to some extent. You can change (or turn off) sounds, select different colors for the table or the deck, even order virtual "drinks" to your seat. It's probably worth tooling around with these options to find a scheme that feels comfortable to you.

RELAX

Unlike when buying a new car, you won't have any problem switching from one site to another if you're unhappy. And you don't have to choose just one. Most pros I know (myself included) have accounts on multiple sites, allowing us to cater to whatever whim we're experiencing that day.

Choosing a Screen Name

When you're playing poker in a brick-and-mortar casino, there is a lot of information available to you about the inner workings of your opponents' minds well beyond the way they decide to play their cards. You can see the way they dress and their posture at the table. You can see when someone's distracted, angry, or drunk. Seat me against a player wearing a plastic watch—usually a sure sign of someone who likes to see the world as an orderly place—and soon I'll turn that world upside down.

Unfortunately, most of this information isn't available to you online. There's no way to know—at least not immediately—if the player you're facing at 7 a.m. is a wild club kid who's been at the table all night or a conservative widow getting an early jump on her day.

One piece of information that *is* available online is a player's screen name. Most of the time, you won't learn much from somebody's handle. What can you really say about a guy who calls himself AcesFull or JohnSmith?

Ironically, screen names are a lot more revealing when they seem to have been chosen to give you a false impression. A player who calls himself 7-2_Offsuit or LoveToBluff wants you to think that he walks on poker's wild side. Miss_Pretty probably isn't a beautiful woman who you can scare off with aggressive betting, and Grandpa_Joe may not be a kindly old man who bets only when he's made a hand. Sure, Jack_and_Julie_Johnson *might* be a married couple sharing the same account, but the name could just as easily be a cover for a college student who wants to leave you wondering if you're playing (please forgive the stereotypes) a formidable and tricky husband or his sweet-natured wife.

While you may not be able to get an honest sense of a player's style from these types of screen names, they do provide you with a piece of incredibly valuable information: These are players who are paying attention to what their opponents think of them, or what poker people call "multilevel thinking" (more on this later). My basic rule is that you can often rely on them, at least at first, to play in a way *exactly opposite* of whatever stereotypical personality trait their name supposedly reveals.

Keep this in mind when you're choosing your own name. Being "tricky" isn't always the best way to trick somebody.

One other piece of advice concerning names: Don't use the same name across multiple sites. While it might not be a big deal when you're starting out, it can be a costly mistake if and when you decide to start multi-tabling across more than one site. If I see PlayerX engaged in six different games across three different sites, I can pretty much guarantee that he's not playing any of them with his full attention. I'm going to look for any opportunity to play against a distracted opponent, preferably in a *shorthanded* or *heads-up* setting.

Making Your First Deposit

You've finished your test-drives, chosen one (or three) sites where you think you'll be comfortable, and filled out the online registration forms. But in order to play for real money, you're going to have to make a deposit. A trip to the site's cashier will give you a variety of options for doing so.

The fastest and easiest way would be to use your credit card—if only it worked. While nearly every site is equipped to handle Visa and MasterCard, most credit card companies won't allow you to deposit money into an online site. The U.S. government—at least at the current time—hasn't quite figured out what to make of online poker.* Since every site is based in a country other than the United States, there's little the American government can do to regulate the industry (i.e., collect tax revenue), so it has put the pressure on the credit card companies not to participate. While this may change in the future— several European cardrooms have recently enjoyed very successful public stock offerings—for now you're going to have to find another way to fund your account.

Fortunately, the need has been filled by a growing number of online payment sites such as Neteller. Without sounding like a commercial— trust me, I don't own stock, although I wish I did—these sites represent the easiest way to transfer money between your bank account and your online poker account. You'll usually have to pay a fee if you want to start instantly, but if you're willing to wait a few days, you'll see that each of these companies offers ways to make transfers that won't cost you anything.

*We'll address the legality of online poker a little bit later in this chapter.

> **Many online poker players use Neteller to transfer money directly between their online and bank accounts—it's free, secure, and usually only takes a couple of days.**

I don't blame you if the idea of giving some online company access to your checking account makes you nervous. It definitely freaked me out at first, so much so that I opened a separate checking account just for online transfers. That way, if someone does manage to hack into my account, all he can steal is my poker money. Whenever the poker account starts to swell, I just write myself a fat check to deposit into the safely inaccessible account where I keep my other money.

And I'm happy to say that, as of today, any paranoia I've had about making these transactions has proved to be just that—paranoia. I've made hundreds of online money transfers and never had a single problem. Neither have any of my friends. These companies live and die by their reputations, and it would take just one misstep to send the customers fleeing.

Is Online Poker Legal?

Online poker is everywhere you look. There are commercials on TV and advertisements in major magazines. Every top pro seems to be affiliated with one site or another, slapping logos on their hats, shirts, and jackets. Virtual casinos sponsor brick-and-mortar tournaments, poker cruises, and fund-raising drives for charitable causes. Many sites are operated by companies that are publicly traded on major world stock exchanges.

Look a little closer at the TV commercials, however, and you'll usually see a disclaimer that the ad is not for, say, PartyPoker.com but PartyPoker.*net*, and says something like "This is *not* a gambling website."

So is online poker legal?

The Department of Justice says no, citing a legal action that was enacted nearly 50 years ago to prohibit people from using their telephones to bet on sports. But no one has been prosecuted under this act to date. In fact, it's not even clear who would *be* prosecuted: Are the sites to blame or the players using them? Furthermore, the entire situation gets even more muddled by the fact that the major online cardrooms aren't based in the United States, but in countries outside American legal jurisdiction.

One beneficiary of the confusion has been Antigua and Barbuda, a tiny Caribbean nation that at least several dozen online gambling sites call home. In 2003, the United States complained to the World Trade Organization, demanding that these sites bar Americans from using them. The WTO initially ruled in favor of the islands, which successfully argued that the U.S. request would violate an already-existing global trade pact, but an appellate body overturned that decision. The sites, however, are still allowed to operate.

The legality of online poker remains a developing situation. The United States has vowed to appeal the WTO's decision. But there's a basic fact the government can't ignore: Online poker has grown into a billion-dollar industry. That's a lot of cabbage, and it seems like it will only be a matter of time before the powers that be figure out how to adjust the laws to get their hands on a share of it.

In the meantime, you can comfort yourself with the words of business and gaming lawyer Chuck Humphrey, who believes that "in today's tolerant atmosphere, the risk of being charged with a criminal misdemeanor is far less than the chance of getting a speeding ticket, and the actual penalty to befall anyone who is charged will be not much more serious than that ticket." Or as law professor and my fellow *Card Player* columnist I. Nelson Rose wrote, "Probably 20 million Americans make technically forbidden wagers each year. With odds like that, you are more likely to be elected governor of California than charged with illegal gambling."

While the legality of online poker in the United States is a developing situation, no one has ever been charged with a crime. Given the minor nature of the offense and the numerous ambiguities surrounding both the law and its enforcement, no one is likely to be charged in the foreseeable future.

How Do I Know It's Not Rigged?

When I tell people I play online poker, they usually respond with the same question: Do you *really* feel secure playing poker over the Internet?

Could it be rigged? Will I take more bad beats online than I do in a casino? Is it true that there's a "cash-out curse" that will cause me to lose for three straight sessions if I'm stupid enough to withdraw money from my account?

The answers are, in order, no, no, and no.

I have played hundreds of thousands—maybe even millions—of hands of online poker. I know plenty of other players who have played as much as if not more than me. And I can't think of a single case where someone has been screwed by the site itself.

"By the site itself"? Am I saying there are ways to get ripped off by other players? What's to prevent two (or more) players from collaborating at the table? Well, actually, there are plenty of safeguards to prevent this kind of cheating. I'd even argue that it's a lot harder to collaborate online than it is in a real casino.

For instance, say you're seated at a table in your local cardroom when it dawns on you that two players—let's call them Bob and Billy—might be collaborating. You call over Old Joe the Floorman and share your suspicions.

What can Joe do? He hasn't seen any of this alleged cheating, which is bound to stop the moment he walks over. He could use the "eye in the sky" to watch their behavior, but without knowing what their cards are, Joe has no way of distinguishing a sketchy play from a legitimate one. Furthermore, if Billy and Bob are regulars, Old Joe isn't going to want to take the chance of insulting two good customers. Your best-case scenario is that a couple of other players complain about their behavior, and Bob and Billy receive a mild warning.

Now imagine the same scenario online. You shoot an e-mail about Billy and Bob to customer service. In this case, whoever's in charge of online security—Internet Ivan—actually has some powerful tools at his disposal. He can monitor their behavior, past and present, with full knowledge of the cards that they're holding. He can study their hand histories, looking for patterns in the way Billy and Bob have played whenever they've been at the same table. And if there's even a hint of suspicious activity, he can not only bar them from the virtual cardroom

> **It may be possible to cheat at online poker, but it's a lot harder than cheating in a live setting.**

but confiscate whatever money they have in their accounts and return it to the players who have been victimized by their deceit.

Who would you rather have on your side, Old Joe or Internet Ivan?

Online cardrooms are constantly on the lookout for cheating of any kind, analyzing each and every hand for suspicious patterns. But wait—that's not all. Some of the more classic ways of being cheated at the table—chip smuggling (where one player surreptitiously slips his tournament chips to another player), marking or otherwise messing with the cards, and shady tournament directors who skim money off the top of the prize pool—are simply impossible to pull off online.

There have been hiccups, of course. In the early days of online poker, one virtual cardroom published the method it used to "shuffle" the deck: The clock on its servers—which measured time down to the millisecond—generated random numbers, which were used to determine which cards would be dealt. The idea was that by sharing this information, the site could soothe any worries about its shuffles being rigged or predictable.

A group of software engineers, however, discovered that they could synchronize the clocks on their computers with the poker site's server and predict exactly which cards would be dealt. While this was bad news for the poker site, it turned out to be great news for the online poker industry. Sites went back to the drawing board to develop new ways to randomize the shuffle. Today's online poker rooms use complicated random-number generators that simply can't be predicted, factoring in things like the fluctuating temperatures of their servers and the way players are moving their cursors.

Another example of improved security can be seen in the way sites address the "timely disconnection" cheat. It's rare in a live casino for a player to become incapacitated—to suffer a heart attack, for example—in the middle of a hand. But Internet users suffer connection problems all the time. In the past, most sites addressed the issue by treating any player disconnected in the middle of a hand as if he were all-in with whatever chips he had already contributed to the pot.

Many enterprising players quickly discovered the benefits of a well-timed disconnection. Let's say that you flop four cards to a nut flush and your opponent makes a huge bet against you. On most sites, if your connection were to "accidentally" go down, the hand would play out as if you had been all-in: You would be eligible to win whatever money was already in the pot should your flush card appear on the turn or river, but you wouldn't have to call your opponent's bet or contribute any additional money to the pot.

Again, sites caught on to this type of behavior. Almost every site limits the number of disconnection-based all-ins a player can experience in a day—anyone exceeding one or two will usually have his hand folded automatically, even if he turns out to have the winner—and online security teams have become more diligent in monitoring this kind of abuse. In one notable instance, several players complained that the winner of a big online tournament had benefited from a suspicious disconnection during its later stages. The site investigated both the specific situation and the accused's playing history, decided that he had indeed disconnected his computer on purpose, and awarded the prize he'd won—a cruise vacation—to the guy who finished in 28th place, the player who had been knocked out of the tournament during the hand in question.

The people who run poker sites know they are one public incident away from losing all credibility and are constantly looking for ways to make their sites more secure. Most have teams dedicated to searching out potential vulnerabilities and improving safety. Some sites have also hired independent auditors to oversee play; others have agreed to the same kind of regulatory oversight used by many of the brick-and-mortar Indian casinos. Almost every cardroom's Web site has a page detailing the various methods it uses to address security issues—reading it may make you feel a lot better.

As far as an overabundance of bad beats or the famed "cash-out curse"—an urban legend in which players who withdraw profits go on to suffer a suspicious streak of bad luck—all I can say is that neither I nor anyone I know has ever seen any evidence of either. If you feel like you're taking more bad beats online than you do in your live games, it's because you are taking more bad beats. Think about it: Where you might see 40 hands an hour in a live game, you might see three times as many (more, if you're playing more than one table) in the same period of time online. Sadly, that means you'll be taking three times as many bad beats. Ouch. The upside is that you'll see pocket aces three times more often.

All that being said, you should immediately report any suspicious activity to customer service. But you'll probably never have to.

Control Your Environment

One huge advantage online play has over brick-and-mortar casinos is that you can do lots of things other than playing poker. You've got your TV and stereo. It's easy to talk on the phone or instant-message your friends. You can surf the Web, get your online shopping done, and catch up on e-mails.

Okay, I'm kidding. While you can do all of these things while playing online, you probably shouldn't.

Keeping yourself free from all these distractions is one of the biggest challenges you'll face. It's way too easy to have the TV on in the background or to play with your dog in between hands. But any time you're focusing on something other than the poker table, you're giving an edge to your opponents. You may be missing out on valuable clues to the way they will play hands in the future, or opportunities to learn a new way to play an old hand. Trust me: Your development as a rising poker star is going to progress much faster if you aren't splitting your attention between the game and Dr. Phil.

Aside from eliminating the obvious distractions, make sure that you're sitting someplace comfortable. Part of being comfortable means that you have a computer and Internet connection that aren't going to slow down or crash at an inopportune time—there's probably no quicker way to go on *tilt* than to get dropped from a game in the middle of a hand you're a cinch to win.

Being serious about your online poker playing doesn't mean you can't take advantage of the comforts of home. If you think you play better when you've got Dokken cranked all the way to 11, then by all means, crank it up! If you want to go without showering for a week, play in your lucky bathrobe, or go naked altogether, hey, it's your thing. Comfortable is the best way to play—it's the No. 1 reason you don't see too many neckties at the poker table.

Johnny Bax

Cliff Josephy, a.k.a. Johnny Bax, was an absolute beginner when I met him. We spent a lot of time chatting online and talking on the phone about basic strategy. Already a rich and successful businessman, he seemed willing to apply the same smarts and dedication to mastering poker.

Today, Johnny Bax is a poker legend. Many sites and player polls rank him as the top online player in the world. He is the poster child for "learning how to learn how to play," a distinction he wrapped up at the 2004 World Series of Poker, where he decided

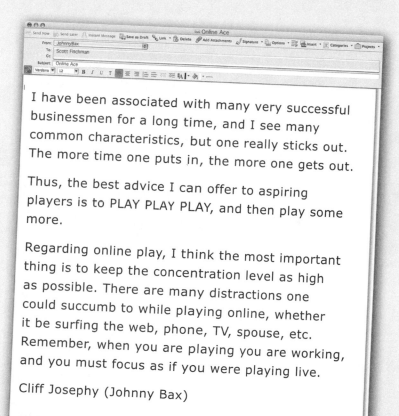

I have been associated with many very successful businessmen for a long time, and I see many common characteristics, but one really sticks out. The more time one puts in, the more one gets out.

Thus, the best advice I can offer to aspiring players is to PLAY PLAY PLAY, and then play some more.

Regarding online play, I think the most important thing is to keep the concentration level as high as possible. There are many distractions one could succumb to while playing online, whether it be surfing the web, phone, TV, spouse, etc. Remember, when you are playing you are working, and you must focus as if you were playing live.

Cliff Josephy (Johnny Bax)

Johnny Bax

to enter the $1,500 seven-card stud event—despite never having played a hand of stud poker. With a five-minute tutorial from a few of his friends—and all the experience he'd earned playing countless hours of online Hold'em—Cliff outlasted 471 opponents to win a gold bracelet and a first prize of almost $200,000. If you are ever lucky enough to watch Johnny Bax in action, pay close attention: You will have the chance to learn from a master.

CHAPTER TWO:
Game Selection and Money Management

I KNOW I'VE ALREADY said this, but it's worth repeating: Poker is a game of decision-making. A player who routinely makes correct decisions will win, while a player who time and time again makes bad decisions will lose, at least over the long haul.

Every player, novice or pro, has to make what might be the most important decision—the one that's going to influence his bottom line more than any other—before seeing a single hand: game selection.

It wasn't long after I started playing serious poker that some friends told me about a game I *had* to play in, a $10/$20 Hold'em game dominated by *loose* players who didn't have a clue. The average pot size was close to $400. It was going to be easy money.

Except that it wasn't. The players were definitely bad—but they were bad in an almost completely unpredictable way. There was no way to tell, for example, if a player reraising over the top of me was bluffing or had really just flopped two pair with the 7-2 offsuit he'd decided was good enough to call the large, pre-flop raise I'd made with pocket kings. I learned the hard way that when five or six players are willing to chase their draws all the way to the river, one of them is usually going to outdraw you. Worst of all, the game totally neutralized one of my favorite skills at the table: creativity. There's no point in trying to pull off an ingenious bluff when no one at the table has been paying enough attention to know he's supposed to fold. As you can probably guess, this game didn't turn out to be quite the cash machine I was promised.

I decided to try my luck at another table, the one all my friends warned me *not* to play. It was a $10/$20 stud game at the Mirage dominated by *rocks* and risk-averse old-timers who got involved only when they held something unbeatable, or nearly so. Rocks are called rocks, by the way, because getting money out of them is like trying to get blood from a stone. The average pot size was something like $50, about one-eighth of what was changing hands at that crazy Hold'em table.

It was almost too easy. When one of the rocks made a bet, I could usually put him on the *nuts* and get out of the way. When I bet, they would get out of the way. Stud can be a very black-and-white game, and these guys were playing by the book. A large-print book. I made creative bluffs at opportune times, gambled when I saw my spots, and absolutely crushed the game.

The moral of the story is that there's a lot more to picking the right game than finding the worst players or playing for the biggest pots. In the crazy game, all I could do was wait patiently for good things to happen to me. In the rocky stud game, I was able to play aggressively, making bets that had a chance of getting the other guy to fold and, in the process, creating my own luck.*

> **The game with the worst players isn't always the best game. It's much more important to find a game you're comfortable playing.**

---

* I'll come back to the whole idea of "creating your own luck" in Chapter Five.

Styles of Play

There are almost as many different ways to play poker as there are poker players. Some people prefer an action game, getting involved in pots with all kinds of hands, hoping to outplay their opponents after the flop. Others like to wait patiently for superstrong hands, risking their money only when they're almost completely sure they've got the best chance of winning. There are players who seem to raise on every hand, and others who prefer to check and call all the way to the river.

With each of these styles come certain advantages ... and disadvantages.

A *loose* player likes to play a lot of hands. As a result, it's often very hard for his opponents to guess what he's holding, occasionally making him the beneficiary of huge pots when his cards combine with the board to make a bizarre straight or unlikely two pair. Unfortunately, the odds of making these big hands are fairly low—at least in the long run—and the loose player is going to waste a lot of money chasing after pots he has little chance of winning.

At the other end of the spectrum, the *tight* player rarely plays a hand. His strategy is to risk his money only when he's holding powerful cards that have an excellent chance of winning. By waiting for favorable situations (and saving his money when the odds are against him), the tight player is usually able to eke out a profit. When he does win a pot, it's often a small one, as his more observant opponents know that it's a bad idea to call his bets. Another downside to tight play is the fact that premium hands don't come around too often—after all, that's what makes them premium hands. It's not uncommon for a tight player to go hours without seeing a hand he considers playable, making for some extremely frustrating sessions at the table.

Another pair of adjectives used to describe players is *aggressive* and *passive*. An aggressive player prefers to control the action, betting instead of checking, raising instead of calling. There are many, many good reasons to be aggressive at the poker table—so many, in fact, that it gets its own section in the next chapter. Aggressive poker can be dangerous business, however, exposing a player to traps from cagey (or even just curious) opponents.

At the other extreme, the passive player will let his adversaries do the betting for him. On the plus side, the passive player won't usually lose too much money on a single hand, isn't very susceptible to bluffs, and will occasionally "suck out" on an opponent with a lucky card on the river. There are all kinds of terrible consequences, though, to this style of play: A passive player can win only when he shows down the best hand, and his refusal to bet when he's ahead allows his opponents to chase potentially winning hands at little or no cost.

Poker players have a nickname for loose-passive players: *ATMs*, as in cash machines. Most authorities on the game will preach the opposite—tight-aggressive play—as the secret to making money with any consistency. Nonetheless, you'll see plenty of seemingly loose-aggressive players making final tables, and there are situations—for example, playing against a total maniac—where tight-passive play may be your best option. The best poker players are able to "shift gears," switching among styles of play to take best advantage of specific opponents or changing table conditions.

Great poker players don't stick to a single style—they shift their styles to suit the specific circumstances of the game they're playing.

Welcome to the Lobby

Your first stop on almost any poker site will be the lobby. If you can resist the urge to jump at the first open seat long enough to take a look around, you'll discover there's an incredible amount of valuable information available worth checking out before you choose a seat.

Every lobby has its own quirks, but most look something like this:

TABLE NAME

Hold'em		Omaha		7-card Stud		Tournaments		
Table Name	Stakes	Type	Plyrs	Wait	Avg Pot	Plyrs/ flop	Hands/ hr
Amsterdam	$5/10	Limit	8/9	0	$70	63%	20+
Bora-Bora	$5/10	Limit	9/9	4	$39	32%	4
Caracas	$5/10	Limit	6/6	10	$60	70%	20+
Detroit	$5/10	NL	4/6	0	$105	71%	20+
El Salvador	$3/6	Limit	9/9	2	$29	29%	5
Frankfurt	$3/6	Limit	9/9	7	$35	70%	20+
Glasgow	$3/6	Limit	2/9	0	$11	82%	20+

Which game should you choose? Let's take a few minutes to decipher all of this information...

While real-life cardrooms almost always refer to their tables by numbers ("Seat open on Table 36!"), virtual cardrooms tend to apply a little more creativity to the naming process, using the names of animals, famous cities, or imaginary streets. In most cases, the table name is purely cosmetic, but there are exceptions. Some sites have deals with famous poker players to host certain games—in other words, take a seat at the Mark Seif table, and you may find yourself playing against the real Mark Seif! Sometimes the name of a table will contain additional information. For example, a tournament table called 100k GUARANTEED means that the site will, if necessary, add money to the prize pool to reach $100,000, while the WSOP $18 QUALIFIER represents a relatively low-priced opportunity to qualify for a bigger tournament whose winner (or winners) will earn entry in the World Series of Poker.

STAKES

In a limit game, this number refers to the size of the small and big bets, i.e., a $3/$6 Hold'em table requires players to bet in $3 increments before and immediately following the flop, then in $6 increments on the turn and river. In a no-limit or pot-limit game, these numbers represent the size of the small and big blinds.

TYPE

This is sort of a catch-all category that provides more information about the game. In the example above, it's used to distinguish between limit and no-limit games.

PLAYERS

This header should be pretty self-explanatory, but there are a couple of considerations to keep in mind. Winning at a shorthanded table usually requires a much different strategy than winning at a full table. As a result, many sites cap the number of players on certain tables—like Caracas and Detroit in the example above—in order to attract customers who prefer shorthanded play.

WAIT

Simply the number of people, if any, who are on the waiting list for a particular table.

AVERAGE POT AND PLAYERS/FLOP

These are probably the two most critical pieces of information that you have available to you, as they clue you in to the types of players you'll encounter at the table. A game with a large average pot size—especially when coupled with a small number of players per hand—tends to be very aggressive, full of raises and reraises. (How else could the pots get so big?) The opposite conditions—small pots contested by lots of players—suggest a passive game with a lot of checking and calling. There's also a direct correlation between the number of players entering each pot and the types of hands they are willing to play:

A high percentage (50 percent or more) indicates loose play; a low percentage means tight.

HANDS/HOUR
This column gives you an indication of how fast a game is moving. A lot of hands per hour (the "20+" means more than 20 hands are being dealt each hour) signifies a fast-paced game, where players are attentive and efficient in their decision-making. A slow-paced game might indicate players who are distracted, excruciatingly thoughtful when faced with a decision, or suffering from a crappy Internet connection. Regardless of the reason, if you're a person who gets frustrated having to wait, you're probably not going to be happy at a slow-paced table.

Choosing the Best Game for You
The type of game you decide to play really depends on what you're hoping to get out of a specific poker session.

Remember the mantra from the previous chapter: It's not about making money, at least not yet. A well-rounded poker education comes from playing in all kinds of games—tight, loose, etc. You want to see firsthand which strategies work best in tight games as opposed to loose, find methods to deal with aggressive and passive players, and develop an understanding of how the value of a certain hand might change with the number of people seated at the table.

You shouldn't be afraid to experiment with a lot of different strategies. This is, by the way, one of the best reasons to start out playing Sit-N-Gos, as a single tournament will expose you to a wide range of constantly changing conditions.

If you're beginning with cash games, however, and want to give yourself the best bang for your buck, you probably want to avoid playing in shorthanded games or facing super-aggressive opponents.

You're going to have to learn to deal with these situations somewhere down the road, but for beginners (and even experts!), there's a much greater risk of losing a lot of money in a very short period of time. Full tables—where you won't feel compelled to play that many hands—populated by passive players probably represent the best opportunity to see a lot of poker while risking a relatively small amount of money.

Take a look at the Frankfurt game in the sample lobby. Most players at the table are seeing each flop, but the average pot size is relatively small—fewer than 12 small bets in every pot—indicating that there's not a lot of pre-flop raising and that most players dump their hands after the flop. Sounds loose, passive, and profitable to me!

Remember that it's critical to feel comfortable, so you're going to want to choose a game whose stakes won't inspire more fear than fun. "Scared money" almost never wins at the table.

As I said in the previous chapter, I like to sit down to a limit game with 30 big bets in front of me. For example, if I decided to play $3/$6 limit Hold'em, I'd buy in for 30 x $6, or $180.

Another good rule of thumb is never to risk more than 20 to 25 percent of your total bankroll at any particular table. I wouldn't choose the $3/$6 table as my regular game unless my starting bankroll was somewhere in the vicinity of $800.

If you're following my "dinner date" advice, you're likely to be starting with a lot less, and should be looking for a lower limit game. For example, let's say you've decided to start with an initial deposit of $200. Since you don't want to risk more than $40 or $50 in any one sitting—which should cover 30 big blinds—your best bet is to start at $.50/$1 (a $30 buy-in) or $1/$2 limits (a $60 buy-in).

If you've decided to start with Sit-N-Go tournaments instead of cash games, you'll want to risk much less of your bankroll on any single tournament. Tournaments with entry fees of around 5 percent of your bankroll sound about right to me.

Keep in mind that these percentages are *fixed*, not relative, to what-ever swings you might experience in your bankroll. Let's say your initial deposit is $200, which you intend to use to play Sit-N-Gos with $10 entry fees. You proceed to finish out of the money in the first 10 tournaments you enter, reducing your bankroll to $100. Unless you feel like you're completely overmatched by the competition, you *do not* want to switch to $5 Sit-N-Gos. Losing streaks are a part of the game.* The key is to play solid poker at the same stakes whether you're winning or losing, giving you the chance to take full advantage of the wins you'll rack up when the pendulum swings the other way.

On the other hand, if you lose 20 straight times, you're probably playing in the wrong game.

One last word of advice about maximizing the value of your early poker education: You don't have to play a hand to learn from it. The tighter you play, the longer your money will last. You'll see plenty of loose players doing their thing, giving you the opportunity to learn from their mistakes—and their successes. Keep an open mind about the various players you'll see, while keeping a firm grip on your chips. Or to put it another way:

> **Be tight in your play, but loose in your imagination.**

Online Etiquette and Idiosyncrasies

Most virtual cardrooms are designed to replicate a live poker experi-ence. Why else, after all, would they deal the cards one by one (when

---

*According to the laws of probability, even a very good Sit-N-Go player—one who finishes in the money 40 percent of the time—is going to run into a five-tournament losing streak about once every hundred times he sits down to play.

a random-number generator has already done the actual work) or use sound effects to simulate shuffling and the click-clack of chips being tossed into the middle of the table?

Obviously there are differences, good and bad, between online poker and the live experience. Online, you're never going to have smoke blown in your face or have to deal with the sounds and smells generated by the guy sitting next to you who just ordered a three-course meal or an in-seat massage. Some differences, however, are a little more subtle and worth a closer look ...

CHAT

All right, maybe this doesn't qualify as a "subtle" difference. Live casinos are full of voices covering pretty much the entire range of emotions that can be expressed by human beings. Online cardrooms have the chat box.

I don't like to chat when I play. It's not that I'm antisocial—I consider myself a personable guy—but I'm usually too busy playing eight different tables across three different sites to hold up my end of the conversation.

Aside from being a distraction, chatters also run the risk of revealing information about the way they play. Take, for example, the ubiquitous "nh"—online poker's abbreviation for "nice hand." What harm can come from typing in these two seemingly innocent letters?

It's not the letters themselves, but the context. A player who types "nh" is usually looking to convey one of two sentiments to the player who just won the pot: 1) that he actually played the hand nicely, successfully deceiving the message originator, or 2) that he played the hand like a complete moron (at least in the eyes of the guy who lost), earning the virtual equivalent of sarcastic applause.

In either case, the player who typed "nh" has revealed something to the rest of the table. If he's being sincere, then everyone now knows he fell into whatever trap was set for him, a potentially valuable piece of information moving forward. This player is either prone to falling into a certain trap or will be overly sensitive to falling into the same trap the next time the situation arises. If he's being sarcastic, then he's probably angry, or at least on his way. While angry people are usually no fun in real life, angry poker players are your friends. They make bad decisions. They have already decided that this day is going to suck. It's your job to help them meet those expectations.

I'm not saying that you should never chat. Many online players are very good at wielding that little text box as a weapon. They can elicit information from their opponents about their playing style. They can foster a sense of camaraderie that occasionally encourages certain opponents to "softplay" against them, declining to insert an extra bet or raise so as not seem impolite or greedy. They can use mockery to push emotionally vulnerable players over the edge, turning otherwise sane people into frothing maniacs. (By the way, if you happen to be one of those people inclined to become a frothing maniac, most sites offer the option to block messages from specific players, or turn chat off altogether.)

A side note about using the chat box to insult other players: This technique works most effectively on good players, or at least players who think they're good. Using chat to berate a bad player is almost always a mistake. What possible gain can come from insulting bad players? By confronting them with their own insecurities, you are essentially begging them to become more conscious of their mistakes, to become smarter. You may even drive them to leave the table! While it may be hard to resist the temptation to throw stones after taking your 453rd bad beat of the day, you're rarely going to gain anything other than a small, inconsequential sense of self-satisfaction, and you stand to lose something much more valuable: a *fish*.

Regardless of whether you decide to chat, you should at least be familiar with the basic vocabulary:

nh	"Nice hand"; "vnh" when it's a *very* nice hand. Often meant sarcastically.
ty	"Thank you"; "Tyvm" when you really want to thank someone "very much."
yw	"You're welcome."
wp	"Well played." The more sincere version of "nh." Can also be "vwp."
np	"No problem."
lol	"Laughing out loud." It's up to you to determine, given the context, whether or not they're laughing at you or with you.
rotfl	"Rolling on the floor laughing." Used to convey a very hearty laugh.
lmao	"Laughing my ass off." Can be combined with the above to make "rotflmao," the nuclear option in cyberspatial humor.
brb	"Be right back." When a player has to step away from the game for a minute or two.
gl	"Good luck." We all need it.
gg	"Good game." A personal favorite of mine. What started as a declaration of good sportsmanship—a player busting out of a tournament shaking the proverbial hand of a worthy adversary—has become the metaphorical equivalent of a kick in the groin. Nowadays, you're less likely to hear "gg" from the victim than you are from the happy survivors who are glad it wasn't them.
nld	"Nice laydown." Used to congratulate an opponent for making a difficult decision to fold a hand or, with dripping sarcasm, to tease a player for folding a hand he shouldn't have.
gh	"Good hand." The same sentiment is sometimes also expressed as "gp" ("Good play").
:)	The emoticon used to represent a happy, smiling face. Other emoticons include ;) (winking), :((sadness), and :o (astonishment).
wtf	"What the f---?!" Most chat boxes use software to censor out profanities.
phuck	The censors are no match for a creative mind.
CAPITAL LETTERS	Capital letters indicate screaming. A little screaming can be therapeutic. A LOT OF SCREAMING can be really phucking annoying.
hmug	"How many chips you got?" Useful when comparing notes with a friend.
ll	"Last longer" bet.
ns	"Nice stack!" This one kind of speaks for itself.

stm!	"Send the money!" Also pretty self-explanatory.
OTB	"On the Button." The player sitting in the dealer seat, usually indicated by a white button. Obviously you won't be required to do any actual dealing in a virtual cardroom—the term is used to describe the player whose position at the table allows him to act last on each round of betting after the flop. One's position at the table can also be described using "EP" (early position), "MP" (middle position), and "LP" (late position).
BB	"Big blind." The (usually) mandatory bet that must be posted before the flop by the player sitting two seats to the left of the dealer.
SB	"Small blind." The (usually) mandatory partial bet that must be posted before the flop by the player sitting just to the left of the dealer.
UTG	"Under the Gun." The player seated just to the left of the big blind, who is in the unenviable position of having to be the first person to act before the flop. "UTG+1" is occasionally used to describe the only slightly more enviable seat just to the left of UTG.
"s" and "o"	Many poker players use "s" to mean "suited." For example, "7-6s" indicates a 7 and 6 of the same suit. They will use "o" to signify the opposite condition: "offsuit" (e.g., "7-6o"). But I prefer to get more specific, using "s" to indicate "spades," in conjunction with "d," "c," and "h." A 7-6 suited might be a "7d-6d," while a 7-6 offsuit might be "7s-6c."
ds	"Double-suited." Used in Omaha to describe a hand with two cards of one suit and two of another, giving you two shots at making a flush, for example, "Ah-2h-Ac-Kc."
SNG	"Sit-N-Go." A type of tournament we'll talk a lot more about in Chapter Four.
MTT	"Multi-Table Tournament." A "standard" poker tournament—we'll cover these in Chapter Six.
B&M	"Brick-and-Mortar." Used to describe a physical (as opposed to virtual) cardroom.
HE	"Texas Hold'em." Variations include "LHE" (limit Hold'em), NLHE (no-limit Hold'em), and "PLHE" (pot-limit Hold'em).
O8	"Omaha Eight-or-better," otherwise known as Omaha Hi-Lo (see the appendices for the rules of this and other games). Variations include "PLO" (pot-limit Omaha) and "PLO8" (pot-limit Omaha Hi-Lo).
7CS	"Seven-card stud." Variations include "7HL" (7-card Stud Hi-Lo).
2-7	"Deuce-to-Seven" Triple Draw.

Built for Speed: Automated Play

One of the best things about online play is its blazing speed. A player in a well-paced brick-and-mortar casino game might see 30 or 40 hands dealt in an hour. In a virtual casino, it's not uncommon to see three times that many hands in the same period of time.

Since there aren't real dealers, there isn't any time lost to shuffling or misdeals. Superstitious players can't ask for a new deck or "setup."* Players also have the option of automating certain tasks that would normally be done manually. Using automated features is usually a time-saver—good news, if you're an action junkie like me—but you should be aware of what you're clicking before you click it.

Automated features save you time and stress, but be aware of exactly what it is you're automating.

AUTO-POST BLINDS

This simple little feature probably saves more time than any other. I can't tell you how much time gets lost in a live game reminding players that it's their turn to post the blind. Unless you're planning to leave the table before your blinds come around, you should always have this checked—especially if you're playing on multiple tables. Your fellow players will be grateful.

MUCK LOSING HANDS

If you don't check this box, you'll usually be given the option, at the conclusion of a hand you've just lost, to show everyone at the table

---

*Players in live casinos have the right to ask the dealer to replace all of the decks in play after playing a full round, resulting in a delay of several minutes as the old decks are taken out of play and the new decks are verified. This break in the action can be very, very annoying.

what you just lost with. I'm not a big fan of showing off my hands unless I have to. Other than to express the proverbial sour grapes, there's rarely a good reason to show a losing hand, and lots of reasons not to, like revealing your current emotional state (angry, disappointed) or giving away extra information about the way you play certain hands. Checking this box will not only free you from the temptation to show the hand but save time in the process.

By the way, you're usually also given the option to show off a winning hand when everyone has folded to you. This is generally a *really* bad idea. You're not only revealing extra information about the way you played the hand, but you are forcing your opponents—especially if you are showing down a bluff—to put you on a wider range of hands. While appearing unpredictable to your opponents might seem like a good idea, it comes with a nasty by-product: You may be unintentionally forcing your opponents to play more unpredictably against you.

I'll admit there are exceptions, however. If you're playing (and winning) a lot of hands, you may want to show a powerful hand every once in a while to let your opponents know that you're not *totally* full of crap. Alternatively, it's occasionally (very) wise practice to show off a bluff just to let the table know that you're capable of bluffing or make an effort to further aggravate an emotional opponent who you think you might be able to knock off-kilter.

AUTO-FOLD

This feature instructs the computer to fold your hand the moment it's your turn to act. I've heard players argue that it's a bad idea, claiming that you reveal to the rest of the table that you are the type of person who will fold certain hands from certain positions, or that you will fold a few hands that you might otherwise reconsider playing given the decisions made by the opponents who have acted before you. Maybe so. But if you're multi-tabling, using auto-fold is almost a necessity—

if you're sure that you're not going to play the hand you've been dealt, click the box and move on to another hand at another table.

AUTO-CALL, -BET, AND -RAISE

Many sites allow you to automatically call, bet, or raise when it's your turn to act. I can't think of a single reason I would use this feature. If I can't pay enough attention to a hand to wait for my opponents to act before deciding whether to call, bet, or raise, then I probably shouldn't be in the hand.

SIT OUT NEXT HAND

Unlike in a live casino—where you can call for "time" to make a difficult decision—you will always be on the clock in an online casino. That being said, it still seems like it takes *forever* for the computer to fold a player who, for whatever reason, has taken his attention off the game. If you know you're going to miss the next hand to go to the bathroom, make a phone call, etc., the courteous thing to do is to check this box. You'll have plenty of time to uncheck it should you get back in time to see the hand.

HAND HISTORIES

One of the more valuable tools available to online players is the ability to request hand histories: e-mailed, play-by-play accounts of specific hands. You can use these histories to help analyze your play after a game or tournament, or to lodge a complaint with the site over the way a hand was resolved.

Many sites allow you to skip the e-mail part and view the previous hand immediately upon its conclusion. This "instant hand history" feature becomes especially important when your opponents call your bet on the river, but, having lost, muck their hands before you can see them—the hand history will usually let you know what cards they were holding, providing you with extra information about the way your opponents like to play their hands.

STATS

Almost every site allows you to keep track of certain statistics regarding your play. Here are a few of the more useful ones:

Percentage of flops seen

You may think that you're a tight (or loose) player, but this number is the proof. There's no "right" answer to how many flops you should see; this number will vary as you experiment with different styles of play against different numbers of players. If you're playing mostly heads-up or shorthanded games, you may wind up seeing 50 percent or more. That same number in a nine-handed ring game, however, probably means you're playing way too loose.

Times called from big/small blind

Again, no right or wrong answers here, but this figure should give you a sense of whether you are "defending" your blinds too much or too little. When I'm on top of my game at a full-size table, I'm usually not calling more than half the time from the big blind or one-quarter of the time from the small blind.

Percentage you call/bet/raise

A quick glance will show you whether you are playing aggressively (with a lot of betting and raising) or passively (favoring the call).

Pots won at (and/or without) showdown

You are obviously looking for a high percentage here, especially on the hands you actually show down, as they are the hands you've usually invested the most money in. When you are playing solid, aggressive poker, you should be winning a lot more hands *without* a showdown.

Being Your Own Boss Doesn't Make You a Good One

When I started playing online poker, nothing would make me happier than winning $100. So happy, in fact, that even if it had taken me only 10 minutes, I'd log off, shut down the computer, and see what was on TV. Within a few minutes, I'd inevitably find myself glancing back at the computer, debating whether to turn it back on. Sure, I'd think, I'll feel like crap if I lose the $100 I just made, but am I really going to sit here and watch *Oprah*?

Setting "stop-wins," or quitting after you've won a certain amount, might feel like a good way to build your bankroll, but it's a bad idea for a couple of reasons. First of all, you're limiting your upside. I mean, there must have been some reason you were winning, right? Maybe you were on your A-game, or at a table full of terrible players, or enjoying a table image that scared the hell out of your opponents every time you bet. Why quit when conditions are so obviously working in your favor?

> **Stop-wins are almost always a bad idea.**

The second reason is that you're working against your goal. Remember, it's not about making money at this point, it's about learning the game. Your poker education isn't just about learning how to make the right plays, but learning to understand yourself: your tendencies, your emotions, the pitfalls that can knock you off your game. How will you respond to going a half hour without getting a playable hand? Or going three hours without winning a pot? Or having your pocket aces cracked five times in a row? Well, there's only one way to find out ...

I realized pretty early on that playing poker didn't mean that I didn't have a boss, but that I was my boss. And that I wasn't necessarily a good one. I needed structure and schedule if I was going to make a serious go at analyzing and understanding my game. I began to play with an eye on the clock—assigning myself a two-hour shift, say—rather than on the fluctuations in my bankroll.

By the way, while stop-wins are generally a bad idea, stop-losses are actually a pretty good one. Whether you're aware of it in the moment or not, losing tends to affect your play, encouraging you to make decisions that are less than optimal. Just as there may have been very good reasons for winning, there are probably equally compelling reasons for losing—maybe you are exhausted, have had too much to drink, or are simply overmatched by the competition. You will probably discover (the hard way) that it's much, much easier to lose money you've made than to win back money you've lost. In any case, losing two or three consecutive buy-ins is usually a good reason to call it a day.

Stop-losses are generally a very good idea.

Part of being your own boss means being a disciplinarian. Smoking in the bathroom, making out in the hallway, and showing up late for class didn't work in high school; they're not going to work in your online education, either. The more you treat poker like a job, the faster you'll improve.

KEEP RECORDS

Keeping records is tremendously important, especially when you're starting out. Whether it's a detailed spreadsheet or just jottings in a notebook, keep a log of every session:

- Game and location (the site you're on, as well as the physical location where you're playing)

- Limits

- Buy-in

- Starting time

- Cash out

- Closing time

Your results are next to worthless if you can't analyze them and spot patterns. You may discover that you tear it up on Monday mornings, when you're fresh and alert, but struggle when you play Thursday nights. Or that you're making a lot more money playing $3/$6 Omaha than $5/$10 Hold'em. One or two sessions won't tell you very much about yourself, but detailed records of your last 50 will paint a pretty accurate picture of your progress (or lack thereof).

In a sense, this is what it's all about: painting an accurate picture of yourself as a poker player. Poker may very well involve lying to other people, but you've got to be ruthlessly honest with yourself. If I had to guess, I'd say that around 75 percent of all poker players think they're above average. Guess what? *Almost half of them are wrong.* It's too easy to blame a losing session on stupid opponents and bad beats. But when you can look at your records and see that those stupid, bad-beat-delivering opponents have separated you from your money nine out of the last 10 times you've played them, or that you have a tendency to wipe out the results of five winning sessions with a god-awful sixth, then you've learned something about yourself and the way you play. Maybe you're not managing your money as well as you should. Maybe those opponents aren't quite as stupid as you think. Think of yourself as a detective, looking to piece together the clues to solve a mystery.

When you know *why* something is happening, then you can figure out a way to fix it. And that, my friends, is the road to improvement.

Poker Tracker

If the thought of keeping statistics is enough to make your brain start hurting—or if you're just looking for an interesting tool to improve your game—consider using Poker Tracker (*www.pokertracker.com*).

Many of my friends swear by it. The program lets you track your results with incredible specificity, letting you see, for example, how well you do raising from the small blind in shorthanded games. When your session is done, you can replay any hand you've played, learning how your odds and equity change with each card—useful for Hold'em, life-altering for Omaha! You can also download your hand histories from most sites, storing information not just about your own play but how your *opponents* are playing as well.

Exclusive

Without online poker, I could never have made a best friend like Noah Boeken, a.k.a. Exclusive—after all, he lives in Amsterdam.

We met playing against one another online, where our mutual respect grew. Noah's tremendous success as an online player translated into the admiration of the entire poker world when, in 2005, at just 24 years old, he won the Scandinavian Open, the main event on the European Poker Tour.

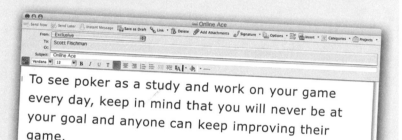

To see poker as a study and work on your game every day, keep in mind that you will never be at your goal and anyone can keep improving their game.

Buy books, watch DVDs, play live games, and discuss and study your results. Never play in a game too big for you … play one that suits your bankroll. Playing online, you can find freeroll tournaments at all sites, a way to grow your bankroll without any risks—check out *www. pokernews.com*, where you can find four to five BIG freerolls a month with $5K prize money and 20-plus smaller events.

Exclusive

CHAPTER THREE:
Basic Strategy

"You're not supposed to make that play."

IT'S A PHRASE I'VE heard many times, especially when I was starting out. Maybe I raised from early position with 9-2 suited or called a tight player's raise in the big blind with Q-10. I'll show down my cards and get a look like I've just killed somebody's dog. If I'm dumb enough to ask what was wrong with the play—hopefully while raking in the huge pot I just won—the answer usually begins with:

"Well, the book says ..."

Don't get me wrong. There are some very good books on poker out there. I know this because people tell me. I just haven't read any of them.

Many of these books—at least from what I've been told—will tell you the "right" time to play K-J offsuit, or the best time to check-raise on the turn. This is undoubtedly useful information, and, I'm guessing, I'd probably agree with a lot of it. I just don't think that memorizing these books is the best way to learn poker.

I saw an infomercial the other night for a video that promised to teach me how to become a pool shark. How am I going to become a pool shark watching videos? Without physically executing the shots—learning the right way to apply English or the touch needed to make the ball carom the right way off the bumper, how am I really going to improve?

If you're anything like me, you don't learn things by reading them, but by experiencing them. You touch a hot stove, you figure out pretty quickly it hurts. Sure, it might be "wrong" to call pre-flop raises with a hand like A-9 or K-Q, but until you've lost a couple of big pots with these hands in situations that you never should have exposed yourself to in the first place, the lesson's not likely to stick.

As a reasonably competent adult, I am no longer afraid of stoves. I eventually learned, as I'm sure you did, that touching the stove will not *always* hurt. I figured out that there are certain principles governing stoves—like, say, they only burn when they've recently been in use—and I developed a few strategies for figuring out when I was at risk of being burned. Another downside to playing the "by the book," especially when you're starting out, is that you may cut yourself off from learning the right time to call a pre-flop raise with A-9 or K-Q—there may not be many situations when it's correct to do so, but they're out there, and they're profitable.

Perhaps worst of all, book-learned play is *predictable*. And predictable is just about the worst thing you can be at the poker table. If you've read that book, odds are so has everyone else. And if everyone knows, for example, that there are only three hands that you'll raise with before the flop when you're under the gun, then you might as well be playing with your cards exposed. And how are you going to make money playing poker with your cards exposed?

> **Against skilled, observant opponents, "predictably" is probably the worst way to play poker.**

I was recently asked whether I'd rather face a final table full of top pros or unknown amateurs. I answered the same way that I think almost every pro would: It's much easier to play against an opponent who always tries to make the "right" play than someone who does things seemingly at random. I'll take the pros—especially the ones who taught themselves to play by reading books—every time.

Most of the great players—especially the older guys, like Doyle Brunson and T.J. Cloutier—didn't learn from books. They learned the game by playing thousands and thousands of hands. This usually involved driving from town to town, state to state, hoping to find a game before the players went bust or the local authorities broke it up. "Road gambling" was the best way to learn how to play poker, but it took years—decades—to master some of the game's more sophisticated concepts.

You're going to accomplish the same feat in a fraction of the time, and you're not even going to have to change out of your pajamas to do it. Thank you, Internet poker.

Without ever having to leave the comfort of your own home, you are going to learn poker the way the road gamblers did: by playing thousands and thousands of hands. And fortunately for you, thanks to virtual cardrooms where you might play 100 (or more) hands every *hour*, it's not going to take you years.

The Factors

Your best strategy, when you're starting out, is to have no strategy. Or better yet, to have every strategy.

If you've seen the coverage of the 2004 World Series of Poker, then you know about the Crew. I was one of a group of guys in their early 20s who stormed the tournament that year, coming from pretty much nowhere to win a few bracelets—including two for me.

When I first met the Crew, I thought I was a pretty good player. I'd played enough poker at that point to have developed a tight, common sense approach to the game that allowed me to be a consistent earner at the table. Which is why, as I started to watch how these guys played, I couldn't believe what I was seeing.

One of them seemed to play every single hand he was dealt. Another appeared to almost never play a hand that wasn't pocket aces or kings. A third gave the impression of being totally unhinged, playing odd hands in even odder situations in what looked to be the oddest way possible. Yet all three had experienced and continued to enjoy a lot of success at the tables.

It was only after months of playing with these guys that I began to see the methods behind their particular madnesses. Player No. 1 was extraordinarily successful in the late stages of tournaments, when the players around him were prone to tightening up. Player No. 2 really seemed to shine in satellites, as he was usually able to preserve his stack in the early rounds with enough chips to survive long enough to earn a spot in whatever bigger tournament he was aiming for. And Player No. 3, I finally realized, was processing each hand like a grand master approaches a chessboard—thinking two and three moves ahead and incorporating some incredibly creative strategies to take down pots.

I began experimenting with these approaches, trying on each of their personas as I entered tournaments. It was only then that I began to understand how each of these strategies had a time and place. Poker tournaments weren't won or lost by sticking to a tried-and-true path but by adopting the right style of play for the right situation.

Good players don't make decisions "by the book"—they look for the options that best fit the situation.

The trick was—and still is—evaluating each situation as I came across it. Every hand is, in some way, unique. But I began to realize that I could break every hand down into Factors: constantly changing snippets of information that combined to define every moment in a game.

HOW MANY CHIPS DO I HAVE?

More important, how will my *stack size* affect my ability to make decisions? Do I have enough chips to play the hand in a way that gives me the best possible chance of winning the pot? This is less important in a cash game—where I should always have enough chips to avoid making "scared" decisions—than in tournaments, where my stack size will affect nearly every decision I make, especially in the later rounds.

WHAT POSITION AM I IN?

This is one of the most important concepts—and maybe most overlooked, especially by new players—for any poker player to consider whether he's playing online or live. Getting to act after your opponents have done so almost always presents you with a huge advantage.

Here's a quick example: You'll hear a lot of players talk about "defending their blinds," calling or reraising opponents who have the audacity to make a pre-flop raise against them. While there are certainly spots where it's appropriate—even necessary—to throw a strong counterpunch from the blinds, many advocates of this strategy ignore a simple but devastating truth: From the flop on, you're going to have to act first on every round of betting.

If you come out betting, your opponent is going to have the chance to raise you if he's strong, or to throw away his cards if he's weak, cutting into your profits. If you don't bet, he can attack you with almost anything (if he thinks you're weak) or opt to take a *free card* (if he thinks you're strong) on the turn that might improve his hand.

Keep in mind that, regardless of what you might be holding, the flop is going to improve your hand *less than half of the time*. With these kinds of odds working against you, it usually sucks to be the guy who has to act first.

"They Might Miss!"

I'm not going to throw a lot of percentages at you in this book, but here's one that Hold'em players should find interesting: The odds of pairing one of your cards on the flop are a smidgen less than 1 in 3.

In other words, the flop is going to miss you more than it will improve your hand. More important, the flop is going to miss your *opponent* in a heads-up situation more often than not.

WHAT IS MY TABLE IMAGE?

Have I just raised four pots in a row without getting a call? Then I should probably have a very strong hand if I decide to raise again, as somebody's bound to think I'm full of crap. The opposite thinking applies if I haven't played a hand in three hours—a raise is probably going to get a lot of respect.

You'll often discover that your opponents, especially in lower-limit games, may not be thinking anything about you—they are too focused on the cards in front of them, what's on TV, or petting their dogs. It's usually pretty difficult, if not impossible, to bluff these kinds of players—they aren't paying enough attention to you to give you credit for the hand you are pretending to have.

But as you move up the food chain, playing against better and better opponents, you'll find that your table image begins to play a vital role in your ability to make money. A maniac may inspire his opponents to call him with almost anything, while rocks scare off the competition with anything resembling a show of strength. A smart "maniac" can use his image to get paid off in a huge way when he actually makes a hand. A shrewd "rock" can pretty much bluff at will.

WHAT IS THE "TEXTURE" OF THE BOARD?

It's not enough to pay attention to your hand. You've got to think about how the community cards might affect the relative strength of your hand by making your opponents' hands stronger or weaker. A♣A♦ is a great Hold'em hand, but you are going to have to play it very differently if the flop comes 5♠6♠7♠ instead of K♠7♥2♣. The *board texture* is an incredibly important Factor in any game with exposed cards. Aside from dictating the "speed" with which you play your hand—how quickly, if at all, you should try to take down the pot—the texture also helps you make an educated guess as to which cards everybody might be holding. A player's actions, when analyzed in conjunction with board texture, help form a "story" about a hand.

Storytelling 🖰

A friend of mine—a very good player who is looking to become a great player—recently e-mailed me about a hand he'd seen at the 2005 Monte Carlo Millions. With a million-dollar first prize on the line and a J♣J♥7♣ flop, Phil Ivey and Paul Jackson got into a raising war, eventually leading Ivey to move all-in and Jackson—who a moment earlier had made a $700,000 reraise—to fold with only $170,000 in chips remaining. It wasn't the aggressiveness or the sums of money involved that bewildered my friend, but the hands the two men were doing the raising with: Jackson held 6-5 offsuit, Ivey an unsuited Q-8. He couldn't understand how the two men, with so much on the line, could risk so much with so little.

I assured him it wasn't drunkenness, temporary insanity, or too much coffee, but a great example of how top poker players use multilevel psychology to tell each other stories.

New poker players tend to make a lot of their decisions based on the cards they've been dealt: "I have pocket aces, so I should raise" or "I've got 7-2 offsuit; I'd better fold." This type of analysis is often called Level 1 thinking.

This new player—usually after taking a series of terrible bad beats—starts to realize that it's not just about the cards he's holding, but what his opponents might have as well. He will begin observing their behavior to make educated guesses about their cards—"putting them on a hand"—and use Level 2 thinking to guide his own decisions.

One day it will dawn on our hero that many of his opponents are just as capable of Level 2 thinking. Level 3 thinking begins when he adjusts his play to incorporate what he thinks his opponents think he's holding. Suddenly, "storytelling" becomes a huge part of the game. He can not only bluff but also engage in elaborate deceptions over the course of a hand that—when they work—will lead his Level 2 opponents to do the opposite of what they should.

Storytelling doesn't stop at Level 3. As analytical players face off, trying to figure out what the other *thinks* that he thinks that the other has, and well, you can see it gets pretty convoluted. So much so that at the game's highest levels, you're sometimes better off flipping a coin.

Let's go back to the Ivey-Jackson example. The flop came J♣J♥7♣. Ivey Jackson led out with an $80,000 bet, as much to gather information as to try and win the pot. Jackson knew this, of course, and raised to $170,000, hoping Ivey would buy his story: I have a big hand.

But Ivey saw a hole in the plot. He knew that Jackson liked to slowplay his big hands, looking to trap his opponents into making big mistakes. If Jackson were strong, he probably would have called Ivey's bet with the intention of raising him later in the hand. Figuring (correctly) that the big raise meant Jackson was weak, Ivey reraised to $340,000.

Jackson, however, hadn't gotten this far by being cowardly. He knew perfectly well that Ivey was capable of this kind of thinking. Hoping to make his opponent doubt his read, he reraised to $700,000, leaving only $170,000 in chips in front of him.

I can imagine Ivey scratching his head. Why would Jackson make a bet that big but leave himself enough chips—what I like to call a "light at the end of the tunnel" stack—to survive if Ivey calls? The obvious answer was that Jackson thought he could lose. He could, of course, be faking the "light at the end of the tunnel" with a really strong hand, but that would be inconsistent with the way he'd played up to that point. Convinced that Jackson's bet indeed meant what he thought it did, Ivey slammed the door shut with an all-in raise. Jackson, having finally run out of storytelling options, did the only thing he could: fold and lick his wounds.

WHAT DO I THINK OF MY OPPONENTS?

Are my opponents the types of players who will "chase" any hand to the river, or are they thinking players capable of folding a decent hand after a big bet or a scary turn card? Is there a lot of bluffing going on? A lot of pushing all-in? Do people seem to be playing "by the book"? This is where creativity and imagination start to become important—if you can figure out how your opponents are thinking, you can start "telling stories" that make sense to them. If your stories are compelling enough, many of them will have very happy endings!

WHAT TYPE OF GAME AM I PLAYING IN?

There are a surprising number of strategic differences between tournament and cash-game play. While getting bluffed into laying down a winning hand can be financially disastrous in a cash game, it's not anywhere near as big a deal in a tournament, where preserving the chips you have is often more important than adding to your stack.

The same goes for limit, no-limit, and pot-limit games. *Drawing hands* that can make you straights and flushes are an important part of limit games but become much more dangerous to play in no-limit games, where an opponent can force you to make a decision for all of your chips before you get a chance to see what the turn or the river brings.

You should also (obviously) be paying attention to how hands gain or lose value in specific games. Getting dealt three aces in a seven-card stud game is reason to celebrate. Getting dealt those same three aces in an Omaha game is usually a good reason to throw your hand away.

The types of players who are sitting at your table can also have a collective effect on the way you should be playing. In a loose limit Hold'em game where six or seven players are entering every pot before the flop, a hand like A-J offsuit loses a lot of its value—you may pair your ace, but a pair of aces is rarely going to turn out to be the winning hand. However, suited connectors (hands like 9♣8♣) or small pocket pairs (which can combine with the board to make trips or quads) are great in these kinds of games, as they not only give you the chance to make a very powerful hand that can win a huge pot, they make it very easy to fold if you fail to improve on the flop.

WHAT ARE THE "STRUCTURAL" CONSIDERATIONS?

This is an especially important factor in tournaments. How big are the blinds and antes? How soon will they be going up? How many players are left? What is the average stack size? How close am I to the *bubble*?

Another important structural consideration is the rake, the small cut that the house removes from each pot to cover its overhead (and generate its profits). The good news is that the virtual cardrooms tend to take smaller rakes than their brick-and-mortar counterparts—after all, there's a lot less overhead to cover. The bad news is that, thanks to the speed of the game, you're going to wind up playing a lot more hands and contributing to rakes more often than you would in a live setting. As you analyze your results, keep in mind that being a winning poker player requires you not only to beat your opponents but also to "beat the rake" as well. Some games, especially at the lowest limits, may be "unbeatable" over the long run, as the money you shell out in rakes will be more than the profits you extract from your opponents.

WHAT ARE THE ODDS?

I know, I promised I wasn't going to make you memorize any odds. And I won't. I think that, on a whole, many players get far too hung up on percentages. Does it really matter whether your chance of drawing to a winning hand is 37 percent or 45 percent? It might—over the long run, if poker were a game played by computers that always made the "correct" play. But in the heat of battle, the odds associated with any specific decision are almost always linked to other variables that are not easily quantified.

> **The mathematical odds of winning a hand are not the only variable to consider. Sometimes, they're not even the most important.**

What are the chances, for example, that my opponent might fold to a big bet or raise? Is there a possibility that my opponent is bluffing? Are there potential *scare cards* that might show up on the turn or river and fool my opponent into thinking that my hand has improved? What if the opposite is true—are there cards that can improve my hand in such a devious and unexpected way that, if I get lucky enough to hit one, I can trick my opponent into making a huge mistake?

Statistics-minded poker players do their best to quantify these scenarios, using concepts like *fold equity* (the chance an opponent folds to a bet or raise) or *implied odds* (to grossly oversimplify, the odds that the odds will change later in the hand). But even the most robotic and calculating player will admit that there are times when you have to rely on instinct. Whatever statistical model you're using might account for the chance that an opponent is bluffing, but your data is going to be, at best, a best guess.

So am I telling you to disregard the whole concept of odds? Of course not. I just don't think a player who is starting out needs to dwell on them. Spend some time seeing how actual hands play out—and how successful players are playing them—before tying your brain into knots over whether or not the guy raking in the pot made the "right" call.

If it seems like I'm not really answering these questions, it's because they're not really questions. The Factors don't have right or wrong answers. They are just things that you should pay attention to when making decisions.

Keep in mind also that while these are some of the most important Factors, this is hardly a complete list. You might notice that your

Odds Calculators

It's worth acquainting yourself with one of the free "odds calculators" available on the Web—you input the hands and cards that are in play, and the program outputs the odds that each will win.

results are different when you play in the morning or at night. Or when you listen to a certain type of music. Or wear a certain shirt. The point is to train your brain to start looking for Factors. Once you've found them, you can start to search for patterns.

Pattern Recognition

I've always been attracted to patterns and structure. If A, then B. Facts float in and out of my brain—somewhere, deep down, I might know the odds of flopping a set when I'm holding a pocket pair, but I probably couldn't tell you if you asked me. But once I understand how something works, it tends to stick with me. I certainly could tell you if, given a situation, it was a good time to play a pocket pair, and what I would do if I flopped a set.

The Factors are the blocks that patterns are built from. For example, you might notice that a player sitting under the gun who makes a minimum raise in a no-limit game often ends up revealing a very strong hand. Or that a player who raises a bet on the flop, then checks the turn, is on a draw.

Patterns will vary from game to game, depending on the type of poker you're playing, the stakes you're playing for, even the time of day you're playing, so it's probably better to start with one game—$3/$6 stud or $10 Hold'em Sit-N-Gos—that you can really zero in on.

Remember that your goal at this point isn't winning or losing but learning. Still, the less you lose, the cheaper your education will be. Here are a few tactics you can use to help stretch out your stake:

PLAY TIGHT ...

You can't lose a pot unless you're in it. If you're paying close attention, you don't have to play a lot of hands to start recognizing patterns—you can simply watch what other players are doing, spotting the ones who are consistent winners and consistent losers. It's almost impossible to play *too* tight when you're starting out. Keep in mind that there are two costs to playing poker—the amount you have to bet or call, and the rake the cardroom is taking out of every pot. The fewer hands you play, the less you're personally going to be contributing to the rake.

... BUT THINK LOOSE!

When I began as a dealer, all I could do was watch other players. A lot of dealers treat their distance from the game as an excuse to shut off their brains—it doesn't matter who's winning or losing, as long as the game maintains a steady pace, the rake gets cut correctly, and the tips keep flowing in.

I've never been very good at shutting off my brain. Every session I dealt was a chance to watch other players, making mental notes of the specific plays and overall strategies that seemed to work. One of the best things I had going for me was the fact that I didn't know enough about the game to be able to judge whether people were playing "correctly" or "incorrectly." All I could do was push the pots to the people who won them. And along the way, I saw a lot of so-called "smart" players lose big and a lot of supposedly "stupid" players win night after night with quiet consistency.

Always try to keep an open mind at the poker table. A lot of what passes for conventional wisdom is actually applicable only to certain situations or, at the very least, can be contradicted by exceptions.

There are times to chase inside straights, bluff a bluffer, or break any other "rule" you may have heard at or away from the poker table. As you watch the players who are winning—I'm not talking about one-session wonders, but the ones who do it week after week—try to separate yourself from prejudgment or emotion and break their games down into Factors. You might be surprised by what you learn.

BUILD YOUR STACK SLOWLY

It's always better to win a small pot than to lose a big one. Poker may seem like a game—especially on TV—where everybody's moving all-in all the time, looking to double their stack on a single hand. Let me tell you, it's a lot easier to build a stack slowly than it is to win huge pots.

Here's another way to look at it: In order to double up in a tournament, two things usually have to happen: You have to have a strong hand, and your opponent has to have a strong hand. Very rarely will you find yourself with the stone-cold nuts—your opponent will almost always have a chance of winning the hand. Most great poker players hate to move all-in for exactly that reason. You can't lose all your chips unless you risk all your chips.

PLAY AGGRESSIVELY

Some players just love to slowplay their hands, passing up opportunities to bet in the hopes of trapping their opponents later in the hand. While slowplaying certainly has its time and place, it's a tactic that a lot of new players tend to overuse. Not only are you giving an opponent a free shot at catching a miracle card to beat you, but you also run the risk that whatever card comes scares him into laying down a hand that he might have called a bet with earlier. More times than not, you're better off betting your strong hands. Sure, check-raising an opponent feels good, but reraising someone who's just raised your initial bet feels even better.

As a rule, it's almost always better to be the bettor. When you call a bet, there's only one way to win: You've got to show down the best hand. If you're the one making the bet, you've earned an additional way to win—your opponent might fold. By the way, this is another great reason to limit the number of hands that you play: When you do make a strong move, your opponents are much more likely to give you credit for having the goods to back it up.

It's usually better to be the bettor.

Carlos Mortensen

If you're at all familiar with the poker world, then Carlos Mortensen needs no introduction—his picture hangs on the wall of World Series champions, he's won a major WPT event, and he's racked up more successful live tournament finishes than there is room to mention here.

But you may not be familiar with what I think is his most impressive accomplishment, and maybe one of the most impressive accomplishments in poker history: winning back-to-back Sunday tournaments on PokerStars, each time defeating a field of more than 2,000 players.

You probably won't recognize Carlos when he's playing online—he uses a variety of screen names to keep his identity secret—but there are plenty of opportunities to watch him on TV. Do so. He is one of the best in the game at reading his opponents.

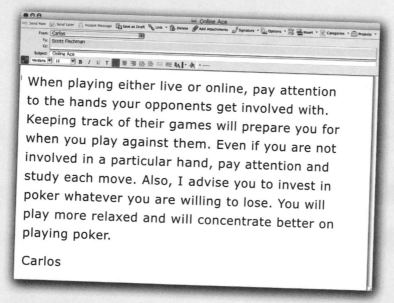

When playing either live or online, pay attention to the hands your opponents get involved with. Keeping track of their games will prepare you for when you play against them. Even if you are not involved in a particular hand, pay attention and study each move. Also, I advise you to invest in poker whatever you are willing to lose. You will play more relaxed and will concentrate better on playing poker.

Carlos

CHAPTER FOUR:
Sit-N-Gos

THERE MAY BE A few shortcuts to learning poker, but there's no substitute for the oldest and most powerful method: playing lots and lots of hands. It's one of the few examples of a situation where addiction can actually improve your life.

So if you've taken the leap and started playing pot-limit Omaha like it's your job, or have dedicated yourself to a regular $2/$4 Hold'em game, well done! Still feeling a few reservations? That's okay too. In this chapter, I'll give you a specific strategy for playing—and winning—Sit-N-Go tournaments, an online miracle that I believe is the best way to learn the ins and outs of poker.*

Sit-N-Gos are unscheduled tournaments, usually confined to a single table (although some sites offer two- or three-table versions), that begin as soon as the table fills up with players. Each player starts with a set number of chips and is eliminated as soon as those chips

---

*I'm going to focus specifically on no-limit Texas Hold'em Sit-N-Gos, but the basic strategy will work just as well in any other kind of Sit-N-Go.

are gone. The blinds go up at regular intervals, forcing players to risk more and more of their chips, creating a sort of ticking clock effect that keeps the tournament from lasting more than an hour or so.

There are several reasons I think they're the greatest training tool in the history of the game:

INSTANT ACCESS TO ACTION

While it may be hard to believe, there was a time when poker players had to wait weeks for a tournament. Nowadays, nearly every site offers them around the clock, so you're never more than five minutes away from a new beginning. Getting knocked out of a tournament on a bad beat doesn't suck nearly as much when you can jump right back into another one.

THEY'RE FAST

You can play three Sit-N-Gos (or more, if you're multi-tabling) in the time it takes you to go to a movie. Their blazing speed allows you to gather and analyze what used to be considered long-term results in a very short period of time.

THEY FIT EVERY PRICE TAG

Most sites offer Sit-N-Gos with buy-ins ranging from $5 all the way up to $100 or more. Better yet, there's a built-in stop-loss—you can't lose more than your entry fee!

EXPOSURE TO CHANGING GEARS

One of the most important skills available to a tournament poker player is the ability to recognize when it's time to "change gears"—mix up the types of hands he plays and the way he plays them. You'll get to experience the full range of shifting gears during the hour it takes to play a single Sit-N-Go.

INTRODUCTION TO FINAL TABLE PLAY

A table in a multi-table tournament looks just like a table in any other game … until you reach the final table. As players get knocked off one by one—pitting you against just a few opponents, a couple of opponents, and, finally, just one opponent—your strategy needs to change dramatically. If you're looking for this kind of experience, it's a lot easier to enter a Sit-N-Go than it is to make a final table!

YOU CAN PLAY MORE THAN ONE

While recent scheduling quirks at the World Series of Poker have forced a few players to play more than one tournament at a time, it's neither easy nor recommended in a live setting. Online, however, is a different story. Drop by my living room on any given afternoon, and I'm probably playing four (or more) at the same time.

IT'S (RELATIVELY) EASY TO MAKE THE MONEY

Most one-table Sit-N-Gos pay prizes to the top three players. In other words, you have to outlast only two-thirds of the field to get into the plus column. By way of comparison, to make the money in last year's WSOP championship event, you had to outlast more than 90 percent of the field.

"Okay, Scott," you're probably thinking, "I get it. Sit-N-Gos are the greatest thing since Velcro. I suppose now I have to go play a bunch of them until I figure out how to win them."

Well, yes. But this time I'm going to arm you with a strategy that will not only help you maximize the amount of time you'll last but put you in a great position to win.

Choosing a Sit-N-Go

Unlike the lobby you used to select a ring game, the Sit-N-Go lobby offers relatively little information. You'll find the types of games and the entry fees, whether they're currently "running" or "registering," and—if they're not running—how many players have already signed up to play. Click on one of the games, and you can watch it in action (if it's running) or choose an empty seat (if it's still registering).

I'll confess a superstition here that, while not necessarily grounded in reality, still helps to put me in a positive frame of mind. Before I choose a Sit-N-Go, I like to take a look at two or three that are already running to find a "lucky seat." In other words, if it turns out that Seat 3 is battling Seat 8 for first-place at one table, and Seat 5 is heads-up against Seat 8 at another, then Seat 8 is obviously the hottest seat on the site. I'll enter the first Sit-N-Go where Seat 8 is still available!

(Yes, I know how ridiculous this sounds, but I'll talk more about positive superstitions in the next chapter ...)

Identifying the Factors

To succeed in any kind of poker, you're going to have to identify and act upon the Factors we've already discussed. Tournament poker, however, adds its own wrinkle to the mix. Because players cannot reach back into their wallets to replenish their stacks, there is a set limit on the number of chips in play. As the blinds increase throughout the tournament, so does the relative value of each chip. In other words, a starting stack of $1,000 might allow you the patience and flexibility to pick and choose your spots when the blinds are $5/$10, but that same $1,000 is going to feel like a lot less when the blinds are $300/$600.

As a result, tournaments can more or less be broken down into three "seasons":

1) The Beginning. You have plenty of chips with which to play whatever kind of poker you please.

2) The Middle. The size of your stack begins to dictate the decisions you are able to make.

3) The Endgame. Many (if not all) of your decisions will be for all of your chips, your tournament survival on the line.

A strategy that works well in one particular season may be completely inappropriate for another. There's not much point, for example, to pushing all-in before the flop at the beginning of a tournament just to win the blinds—why risk so much for so little? Later, however, when the blinds represent a much larger percentage of your stack, pushing all-in before the flop can be an extremely powerful play. In a minute, we'll break each season down, looking for the most effective strategies for success.

But the real trick—aside from getting lucky in the right spots—is knowing when the season is about to change. While I'll give you some criteria to help you figure it out, a lot depends on the structure of the particular Sit-N-Go you're playing. How many chips do you start with? How fast do the blinds go up? How big is the average stack compared with the blinds? You should recognize these types of questions, of course, as Factors, and it might be worth it for you to watch one or two of the Sit-N-Gos you're interested in playing before risking any of your own money.

Perhaps the most important Factor in Sit-N-Go tournaments is recognizing when the "season" is about to change—then altering your strategy to take advantage.

The Beginning

Some people might think of poker tournaments as an amusing pastime. Others may treat them as business opportunities. I like to see them as a great experiment in social theory.

Think about it: Everyone starts with an equal stack. Your fate isn't determined by who you know but by *what* you know. Success takes bravery, cunning, positive thinking, and a little help from a completely impartial higher power—the luck of the draw. Democracy in action!

At the start of the tournament, everyone has plenty of chips in relation to the blinds, allowing them to play as many hands as they please. Let freedom ring! Before jumping in feetfirst, though, you may want to consider that there are plenty of good reasons not to make a move at all.

Here's the funny thing about Sit-N-Go tournaments: It's much more important to win pots later than it is to gather a lot of chips early. This may sound like a fairly obvious statement, but it's actually a very important strategic concept.

At first glance, the reasoning looks pretty simple. The blinds are smaller. Smaller blinds usually mean smaller pots. With less money in the middle to win, there's less incentive to win it.

The more fundamental reason, however, relates to tournament poker's very nature: Players are being eliminated, but the number of chips in play remains the same. Taking this logic a bit further, it follows that the average player remaining in a tournament at the midway point is going to have more chips than the average player at the start. *Doubling up* at the beginning of a tournament may feel good, but it's nowhere near as beneficial as doubling up against a larger stack later on down the line.

Here's another way to look at it: You're going to have to win a lot of pots in the early stages of a tournament to earn as many chips as you will if you win just one or two hands in the middle stages. Which sounds easier to do, winning a lot of pots or winning just one or two?

Now, I'm not saying that it's not a good thing to win a lot of chips early—it certainly makes your life easier in the middle stages. It's just that there's not much reason to put your stack at risk to win relatively small pots at the beginning when you're going to need those chips to take bigger risks later in the tournament.

I've heard some players say the optimal strategy in the beginning of a Sit-N-Go is to fold every single hand. Think about it: Sure, you'd lose a few blinds, but winning just a single average-size pot in the middle of the tournament would more than cover your losses.

I'm not going to advocate playing that tight, but I'm going to come close. My goal in the beginning of a Sit-N-Go tournament is to look for spots where I can safely—or as close to safely as poker allows— double my stack. Otherwise, I've got no business being in the hand.

I'll play any "extra premium" hand, of course—pocket aces, kings, queens, and jacks, as well as A-K—but I'm going to do my best not to go broke with them. If the board looks scary, and someone makes a huge bet into me, I don't have any trouble folding, even if I think there's a decent chance my opponent might be bluffing. Remember: It's much more important just to survive at this point than it is to win pots.

I'll also play—as long as I don't have to call a raise—any suited ace or pocket pair. Why these hands? Because they're *low risk, high reward*. With the pocket pairs, I'll either flop a set—a powerful hand that I'm usually willing to risk all my chips with—or throw them away. With the suited ace, I'll either flop the nut flush or, on rare occasions, flop four cards to my flush and get a free (or very cheap) look at the turn. Note I am looking for the flush and only the flush. If I pair my ace? I'll check and fold to almost any bet.

In other words, I will throw away every other hand I'm dealt. That's right, no K-Qs, no suited connectors, not even A-Q (unless it's suited). I'm not looking to build my stack; I'm trying to double it, and if that fails, preserve it! There's no point in risking my chips on anything else.

Finally, I will never ever bluff in the beginning of a Sit-N-Go tournament. Why bother? There's not going to be a pot large enough to warrant the risk that my opponent can call me with a better hand.

The Middle

Knowing when you've reached the middle of a Sit-N-Go has more to do with the size of your stack than the number of players remaining. As a general rule of thumb, you've reached the middle when your stack is only big enough—whether due to losing, increasing blinds, or both—to cover around eight big blinds.

With more than eight big blinds, I can keep playing pretty much the same strategy I did at the start—low risk, high reward. I will make one significant adjustment if several opponents have reached their Middles (eight big blinds or less) before me: I will lower the size of my opening raise from five times the big blind to two and a half.

Why lower the raise now? Because my opponents are getting more desperate. They don't want to waste chips by calling raises, but they know that the time to risk *all* of their chips will soon be upon them. My smaller raise allows me to take advantage of their desperation without putting too much of my own stack at risk. I can make the 2.5x raise with pretty much *any* hand if I think there's a good chance my opponents will fold. If they "play back at me" with an all-in raise, I can decide to call them (if my hand is strong) or fold (if my hand is weak), escaping without putting much of a dent in my stack. When everything goes well, this strategy allows me to build an above-average stack into a humongous stack that will allow me to sail into victory.

Many days, however, it will be *me* reaching the eight big blind threshold before my opponents do. And when I do, I have to start looking for spots to raise all-in before the flop, hoping to win the blinds without a showdown.

Raise It Up!

In limit poker, raising is easy. You just have to say the words, and the game dictates the amount. In no-limit poker, however, you've got to actually say how much you are raising. And the figure you choose actually *means* something, both mathematically (you can control the odds an opponent is getting to call your bet) and psychologically (deciding to bet half the pot sends a much different message than moving all-in).

While the math is important (for more information, you may want to read the section on *Odds and Outs* in the appendices), I'm going to focus on the psychology. One of the worst things you can do as a no-limit player is tie the size of your pre-flop raise to the strength of your hand, even if you think you're being sneaky about it. When a player makes a minimum raise from early position, for example, I can almost always put him on a very strong hand.

Most players try to make a "standard" raise before the flop, usually around three times the size of the big blind. Though it's a perfectly good number to use in no-limit cash games or a lengthy tournament, the action in Sit-N-Gos tends toward the wild side. It's not uncommon to see a player lead out from early position with a "3x" raise and get called by five or six opponents.

During the Beginning stage of a Sit-N-Go, I like to open with raises five times the size of the big blind. My goal is to avoid multi-way pots: I either want to get heads-up with a chance to double-up, or get everyone to fold, preserving my stack for later. For whatever reason, the same yahoos who won't think twice about calling a 3x raise are a lot less likely to call a 5x raise.

Why do I draw the line at eight big blinds? Because I still have enough chips to put a dent in someone else's stack. The ability to inflict pain is the ability to instill fear. In other words, my all-in raise may still carry enough fold equity to encourage an opponent to lay down a hand I'd rather not face in an all-in showdown.

Despite what you see on TV, most serious poker pros *hate* showdowns. Before the flop, no hand is a lock over any other. Even pocket aces are going to lose once in five tries to most other hands. Those are great odds in a cash game (where you'll be able to reach into your wallet to replenish your stack those times you lose), but potential disaster in a tournament, where you've got only one life to live.

Tournaments are all about survival. When you push all-in before the flop with eight big blinds, you're not just hoping to double up, but you're counting on the very real possibility that you'll simply take the blinds, increasing the size of your stack by (at least) nearly 20 percent!

Fewer than eight big blinds, and the temptation to call you grows far too strong. Let's say, for example, you push all-in with six big blinds. Since there's already a blind and a half in the middle (the big blind and the small blind), your opponent sitting in the big blind only has to call five big blinds to win 7½. If you do the math, he's got to win only 40 percent of the time to make calling your all-in raise a profitable play. He's getting about the right odds to call a hand like A-K with almost any two cards.

The nice thing about pushing all-in while you still have fold equity is that you don't even have to have a good hand. Maybe you're bluffing. Maybe you're not. In a perfect world, your opponents have been paying attention to the fact that you haven't been playing any hands so far and will give you credit for having something this time around.

The key is to find the right situation to push all-in, one that maximizes your chances of *stealing the blinds* without a showdown. Poker players call these opportunities "spots." How do you identify a spot? It's mostly instinct and experience. But here are some things to look for:

YOU WANT TO BE THE FIRST PERSON INTO THE POT

When someone raises in front of you, he's already announced that he's got a good hand. Plus, the money that he has added to the pot improves the odds he (and everyone else at the table) is getting to call you, creating a dreaded showdown situation. Unless you've got a great hand—one that you wouldn't mind reraising with—you're probably smarter if you wait for a better spot.

IT'S EASIER TO STEAL FROM LATE POSITION

With fewer players left to act, the odds of your running into a monster hand are much smaller. But keep in mind that many players will almost automatically assume that any late-position raise is an attempted steal and will "play back at you." Hopefully, you've been paying close enough attention so far to know who these players are and avoid them (unless, of course, you actually have a great hand).

IT'S EASIEST TO STEAL AGAINST AVERAGE-SIZE STACKS

Your short-stacked opponents, who know that time is working against them, are looking for a chance to get all their money into the pot. Your raise might be just the opportunity they're looking for. An opponent with a lot of chips, on the other hand, might be inclined to say "what the hell," calling your bet even if he's got the worst of it in the hopes of crippling or eliminating you. But the average stacks? They feel like they're still in the hunt, often playing a little more conservatively than usual while waiting for spots of their own.

What happens if you can't find a spot? When your stack gets small—say, four big blinds or fewer—you are in "all-in mode." Anytime the action gets folded around to you on the button or in the small blind, you *must* go all in. You should also think about pushing all-in from any position with any ace, pocket pair, or other hand with a reasonable chance of winning a showdown. You still have enough chips to get a weak hand to fold, but you won't for long.

The Endgame

Four players left. Three will get paid. Time to buckle down, tighten up, and survive long enough to make the money, right?

Wrong. Your goal—at least in this particular strategy—is to win the tournament. And the easiest way to win the tournament is to have a lot more chips than your opponents do once you get down to the final three.

Once again, the reasoning is simple. Many (if not most) of the show-downs at the end of a tournament are going to involve all-in situations. The more chips you have, the fewer showdowns you'll have to win to capture first place. Just as important, you can also afford to *lose* more showdowns than your opponents, further shifting the odds in your favor.

To build a large stack, you're going to have to overcome your survival instincts and start playing a style of super-aggressive poker that some might call reckless. I call it the "over the hump" strategy.

Every decision is binary: all-in or fold. The idea is to force your opponents—who, hopefully, will be clinging to their chips in the hopes of making the money—to make life-threatening decisions at every turn. With their lives on the line, most players won't want to gamble with anything but the strongest hands. And as the strongest hands don't come around too often, that usually means folding.

When the blinds get big, there are actually two benefits to winning a pot: the chips you've won, plus the chips you didn't allow your opponents to win. A pre-flop raise that wins $200/$400 blinds doesn't just earn you $600 but keeps $600 out of another player's stack. That's a

$1,200 swing. With enough $1,200 swings, you'll be in great shape to keep rolling forward even if you lose one or two showdowns.

You're going to apply the same criteria as before for picking spots—

When the blinds in a tournament get big, so do the two benefits that come from stealing them— you've grown your own stack and prevented your opponents from adding to theirs.

---

attacking from late position, avoiding other players' raises—with a couple of twists.

One is something I like to call the "hand of God." It may be in your best interest, in certain situations, to keep a weak player alive rather than eliminate him. Here's an example (see page 78):

Everyone folds to you in the small blind. Your instinct might be to raise with just about anything to knock Player C out of the tournament.

But what happens once Player C is gone? Players A and B, having happily made the money, will probably loosen up. Your aggressive edge has been eliminated. And while you might have the most chips now, you won't if you lose just a single showdown.

Here's where you use your "hand of God." Fold and let Player C survive. So what if he doubles up? Let Players A and B worry about eliminating him. As long as C is around, they're going to have to fold to most of your all-in raises. Momentum is still on your side.

This might look like cheating to your opponents, but it's actually a real money decision. You will have the most leverage in attacking A and B while C is still alive.

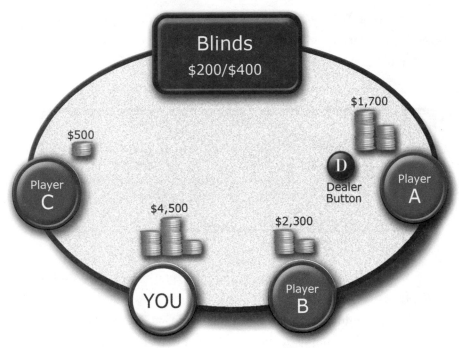

With a more dominant chip lead over Players A and B, your strategy flips. (See page 79.)

In this situation, you don't mind taking on Players A and B. You have enough chips to ensure that they are going to have to double up against you more than once in order to knock you out of the lead. You already have to post $200 in the small blind; losing another $550 won't have any significant effect on your chip lead. If Players A and B fold, giving you the opportunity to go heads-up against Player C—who already has to spend more than half his chips just to pay the blind—you should consider going all-in with almost any two cards. You're getting great value for your money if Player C calls—you've already put in $200 posting the small blind, so it's just another $550 to buy a shot at winning a $1,500 pot—and there's still a chance, however slight, that he might fold.

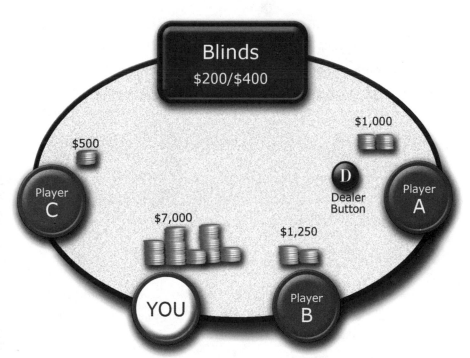

Eventually, the bubble is going to break—someone will get eliminated. Your opponents are now going to be more relaxed, and recklessness isn't going to work as well as it did. You're still going to push all-in when you think you've got a spot, but you're going to be facing a lot of decisions as to whether or not to call your opponents' all-in bets.

More often than not, calling all-in bets when you have the chip lead is a bad idea. The true power in having a chip advantage at this point in the tournament is your ability to be more selective in the hands that you play. You might be tempted, when you look down to find a hand like A-4, K-J, or 4-4, to call an all-in bet, especially if you're in the big blind. But depending on your position, you'll rarely be anything more than a slight favorite in this situation, so why take the chance?

Of course, there are situations where you'll call. You may have a premium hand of your own. Your opponent may be so short-stacked that doubling him up won't affect your lead in any significant way. But I can't stress it enough: It's much better to be the guy pushing all-in than the guy deciding to call. The aggressor has two ways to win—a showdown or a fold. And as the prize structure of most tournaments rewards second place with substantially more money than third place—there's still plenty of incentive for your opponents to fold.

Do your best not to get too emotional about the outcome of any individual hand. If you've built a chip lead during the "over the hump" period, you're going to have to lose more showdowns than your opponents to lose the tournament. They are going to have to get luckier than you. It will happen, of course, but thanks to the laws of probability, it *probably* won't.

You may discover that use of this Sit-N-Go strategy will result in a lot of first-place finishes ... and a lot of fourth-place finishes. That's okay—given the structure of most Sit-N-Gos, it's better to win once than to earn three third-place finishes.

Keep in mind also that if your opponents are savvy enough to know what you are doing (or if you recognize an opponent using this strategy against you), they will start playing more aggressively against you, forcing you to make all-in decisions. It's one of the reasons I sometimes change my screen handle or use different accounts against opponents who know who I am and how I play.

I've seen people build lives with this strategy: not just bankroll, but experience and confidence that can carry over into bigger and bigger tournaments. Here's hoping it works for you, too.

Michael "The Grinder" Mizrachi

I met The Grinder—along with his brothers E-Wee and Rob, and the rest of their Florida crew—in Tunica, my first trip to a major tournament. We were young, barely solvent, and incredibly determined to get better. We immediately became friends.

Today, Michael is a superstar. If you're a fan of televised poker, you've seen him win some huge tournaments. I can tell you he's probably earned just as much money online, winning the big PokerStars Sunday tournament (and making the final table at least five times). It has been an absolute pleasure watching Michael enjoy the kind of success that he has.

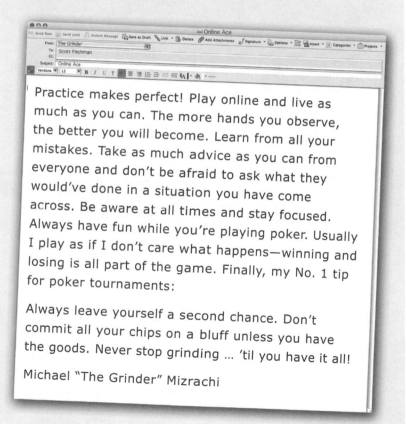

Practice makes perfect! Play online and live as much as you can. The more hands you observe, the better you will become. Learn from all your mistakes. Take as much advice as you can from everyone and don't be afraid to ask what they would've done in a situation you have come across. Be aware at all times and stay focused. Always have fun while you're playing poker. Usually I play as if I don't care what happens—winning and losing is all part of the game. Finally, my No. 1 tip for poker tournaments:

Always leave yourself a second chance. Don't commit all your chips on a bluff unless you have the goods. Never stop grinding ... 'til you have it all!

Michael "The Grinder" Mizrachi

Michael "The Grinder" Mizrachi

I have tremendous respect for Michael's game, especially when it comes to heads-up play. I have to credit him for helping me improve that aspect of my game, even though I had to beg him to do it!

CHAPTER FIVE:
Intermediate Strategy

GOOD NEWS, BAD NEWS

The good: Your probationary period is coming to an end. You've (hopefully) been putting in the hours at the table, seen several thousand hands won and lost, and developed a few ideas about how the game should be played. You're ready to elevate your game to the next level.

The bad: You will receive a grade. And at the poker table, there's only one way to keep score. It's time to start winning some money.

Winning Poker Isn't About Winning Pots

The player who wins the most pots is not the best player at the table. He may, in fact, be a *losing* player. The goal is not to win a lot of pots. The goal is to win a lot of money.

There are two equally important aspects to being a winning poker player:

1) You maximize your winnings.

2) You minimize your losses.

This may sound totally obvious, but you'd be amazed how many people sabotage their earning potential by ignoring one or both of these aspects.

Maximizing Your Winnings

This is, for most players, the easier of the two concepts to address—much of the rest of the chapter will be dedicated to strategies you can use to make sure that you are doing the best you can to milk every bet possible out of the pots that you win.

As you read on, however, keep the following idea in mind: Winning poker, especially at the beginning and intermediate levels, is usually not sexy.

If you've ever played blackjack, then you're probably familiar with the concept of counting cards. The basic idea is that by keeping track of the cards that have been exposed, you can try to predict which cards will come. This knowledge allows you to make seemingly odd bets—either larger or smaller than usual—when you know that the deck is working for or against you.

While casinos hate good card counters, they *love* bad ones. As it turns out, a would-be card counter who makes just a few mistakes is probably going to lose more money than a non-card counter using basic blackjack strategy.

Poker works the same way. A lot of the game's more creative concepts—bluffing, slowplaying, check-raising, limping in with big hands—can actually cost you money when used too often or in the wrong spots. Most of the money you make at the poker table will come from betting or raising when you think you have the best hand.

Minimizing Your Losses

Just as important as the things you do are the things you *don't* do.

One poker truth you may have encountered by now is that it usually takes much longer to win money than it does to lose it. A day of solid play can be wiped out by one or two mistakes. You played a hand you just knew you shouldn't have played, called a raise when you were sure you were beat, or tried to bluff an opponent you had no chance of driving out of the pot.

> **Avoiding losing situations is as important to your bottom line as maximizing your wins.**

There is no shame in folding when you think you have the worst of it. Late in an online tournament, I will often pretend I was in the bathroom and missed my turn rather than play a hand that I know has a good chance of getting me into trouble.

Not that I do a lot of backpacking, but I've heard an expression used by people who do: "Ounces make pounds." One or two extra items may not break your back, but they add up in a hurry. The same rule applies at the poker table. Calling the occasional raise, spending a half-bet to play junk from the small blind, or limping in with a weak ace may not cost you much in the moment, but it doesn't take too many moments to turn a winning player into a loser.

How Much Should You Expect to Win?

I've heard players talk about how much they "should" win at the tables. "One big bet per hour" is a popular answer.

I disagree, not necessarily with the answer, but with the question itself. There is no "should" in poker, except for the all-important notion that you *should* always be making the best decisions in whatever game you find yourself playing.

I understand why people would want to have an idea of how much they should expect to win. We all have expenses in our lives, and it's only natural to want the security of "knowing" that we're going to earn $500, $5,000, or $50,000 this week.

Obviously, poker doesn't work that way. It's nearly impossible to predict one's success. Games change, bad players drop out (or get better), and luck—good or bad—can play a much larger role than most players like to admit.

Aside from the fact that you probably won't be able to forecast your winnings with any accuracy, there is an even better reason to avoid this kind of thinking: What good can come of it?

If you exceed your expectations, you may wind up setting your sights too high. Failing to meet your expectations can sabotage your positive mind-set. And meeting your expectations, while reassuring, might prevent you from recognizing a few *leaks* in your game—what if you've set your expectations too low?

I was asked in an interview, after my success at the 2004 World Series of Poker, about my expectations for 2005. I answered that I expected the field to be about four times larger and that I anticipated making more money than I lost. To expect anything more would have been setting myself up for failure. Better to be pleasantly surprised than even moderately disappointed.

Keep your expectations positive but modest, leaving plenty of room to surprise yourself with the upside.

Stop-Wins, "Squirrels," and "Hit-and-Run Artists"

I used to play in a game whose regulars included a guy named Marty. Marty always wore a warm-up suit to the table, not because it was comfortable (although I'm sure it was) but because he was actually warming up.

Marty's single-minded goal at the poker table was to get to the gym as quickly as possible. Each day, he played until he was up $100, pocketed his winnings, and headed off to begin his workout. Sometimes it would take him less than five minutes. Other times his chance to get some exercise disappeared along with his chips.

To his credit, he'd apparently survived on this strategy for 20 years, so he must have been doing something right. But it was apparent, to me and everyone else at the table, that Marty was also doing something wrong: He was setting an artificial stop-win for himself.

Sure, he was making a few hundred dollars a week. A guy with Marty's skill, however, could have been making a few *thousand* dollars a week while spending even less time at the table (and more on his workouts).

It's easy to understand Marty's thought process: If I lock in my winnings, I'll always be a winner! What he failed to account for was that the easiest time to win money at poker is when you are winning.

Winners tend to play with confidence, which breeds more winning. Their frightened opponents often wind up playing a little more conservatively, playing fewer hands than usual or missing bets that they should have made. Plus, there are two factors often associated with winning that should always be exploited when you have the chance: You are playing good poker and you are playing against opponents you can beat.

The other failure in Marty's strategy is that it put him in a situation to win a little ... and lose a lot! On his best days, he won $100. On his worst days, he might lose $1,000. In other words, he'd have to enjoy 10 straight good days to make up for one really bad one.

In the world of online poker, the Martys out there generally take the form of *squirrels* or *hit-and-run artists*.

Squirrels buy into a game for the minimum amount. They play until they win a hand or two, leave the table with their winnings, then reenter the game with a minimum buy-in, having "squirreled" away their earnings.

The problem with squirreling is that it often forces you to play short-stacked poker. A squirrel who loses an early pot or two usually finds himself in a position where he has to go all-in with his remaining chips in the middle of a hand. This might not seem like a terrible strategy—a player who has moved all-in might lose less from a *suckout* on the river and may get to see one or two cards for "free," engineering a suckout of his own—but the squirrel will ultimately wind up costing himself money. Not only is he missing out on the chance to collect the bets made on later streets (which are usually much bigger than the bets made earlier in the hand), he's sacrificing the opportunity to push opponents out of the pot with big bets or raises, allowing them the chance to draw out against him.

A squirrel's close relative is the hit-and-run artist. Tell me if this sounds familiar: An opponent—usually after delivering a terrible beat to win a big pot from you—quickly exits the table, sometimes logging off the site entirely. There aren't many more infuriating experiences. But while hit-and-run players might really piss me off in the moment, I'll eventually find solace in the fact that, by limiting their wins, they aren't earning as much money as they should.

The moral of the story is simply that good players—those who consistently make bets when they have a positive expectation and fold when they don't—will cost themselves money by setting artificial limits on their wins. And in poker, missing opportunities to win money can be just as devastating as finding opportunities to lose.

Taking Notes

Now that you've been playing online for a while, you're bound to have bumped heads with some of the same players over and over again. Maybe you've even started to spot a couple of tendencies—GreenBud420 will play any two cards, Bluffer666 is surprisingly tight. While you're still focused on identifying the patterns that will help you beat *every* opponent, you're pretty sure there are a few exceptions that will help you beat *specific* opponents.

All poker players keep a book—whether actually written or stored in their heads—on how certain opponents have played them in the past. There might not be anyone better at this than T.J. Cloutier, who will remember that you slowplayed a set against him ... in 1986.*

Keeping track of other players can be a pretty tough task if you play a lot of live poker, even more so if you're playing online, where you'll cycle through opponents at a much faster rate.

Fortunately, almost every online cardroom allows you to keep notes on other players. It's a really handy feature. When I first sit down to any game, I quickly look over the other players at my table to see if I've gathered any information on them in the past.

There is an art to note-taking—you want your notes to be useful. Jotting down "This guy SUCKS!" after he delivers you a terrible bad beat may make you feel a little better, but it's not likely to help you in the future. How, specifically, did he suck? Is it possible he was drunk while playing? Was he talking smack all night? Or is he a newbie learning the game, in which case he's much less likely to suck the next time you play him?

As you can see, it's tough to make meaningful, useful observations about the quality of someone's game, especially online. What you can do is make a note every time a player makes an out-of-the-box play.

Limping in with a big pocket pair is an out-of-the-box play. So is an abnormally large raise—say, 10 times the big blind—before the flop.

*It's also one of the reasons why T.J. may not have benefited from the poker boom as much as some other pros—the constant influx of new, unfamiliar, and unpredictable opponents puts a huge crimp into one of his greatest strengths as a player.

Maybe it's a check-raise bluff on the turn. The key is to be as specific as possible, identifying a situation that might come up again during a hand you're involved in, while keeping the note simple enough to provide relevant information in the heat of battle.

TYPES OF PLAYERS

Most of us grow up learning that it's wrong to stereotype people. At the poker table, *not* using stereotypes can be a huge mistake.

First off, let me be clear that I'm not talking about judging players by their race, gender, or educational background—there are plenty of great players (and awful ones) from all walks of life.

There's nothing wrong, however, with stereotyping players by their style of play.

Keep in mind that most players won't fall neatly into these categories—a maniac may only be a maniac when, say, he's drinking—or may exhibit characteristics from more than one category (a player who plays too many hands before the flop might play very solid poker after the flop). The point I'm trying to make is that there's no "right" way to play poker that works every time; you're going to make the most money when you continually adapt to the players you're playing with.

Online Tells

Most of the fictional poker you see in the movies or on TV emphasizes a single aspect of the game: the tell. Whether it's the tone of someone's voice or the way he eats his Oreos, our heroes always seem to be on the lookout for some vital clue that will betray the nature of an opponent's hand. The search for tells has led to countless hours lost to "staredowns" at the table, while the fear of actually having a tell of one's own leads otherwise sane players to wear sunglasses, hats, even hoods to cover their entire heads.

Type of Player	Battle Cry	Characteristics	Counter-strategy
The Maniac	"Raise!"	Will raise with just about any two cards and, with seeming disregard for the board, bet when you check and raise when you bet.	Tighten up. It may seem counterintuitive, as he'll often be playing junk, but your biggest profits will come when you punish him with your strongest hands. It's also okay to call more often than usual, letting him do some of the betting for you.
The "Plastic Watch"	"But the book says ..."	Will always look to make the "textbook" play, betting with the best hand, calling with the right odds.	Try to pay as much attention to odds as he does—he's not going to risk his money unless they're on his side. He's also going to pride himself on making big laydowns, making it easier to bluff him off a hand.
The Bluffer	"You've got to pay to see!"	Will bet whenever he thinks he has a chance of taking the pot with a bluff, which is always.	Be aware that he'll bet into any empty space: For example, if everyone checks the turn, he'll almost always bet the river. You may have to call a few of his bets in obvious bluffing situations if you've got any hand with a chance to win—you don't have to be right very often to make this a profitable strategy. When heads-up against a bluffer, you may find more opportunities than usual to slowplay a big hand.
The ATM	"I call!"	Limps into a lot of hands and will call with nearly any hand that has a chance to win or improve to a winner.	Tighten up. You're never going to be able to bluff an ATM, but you'll more than make up for it when he pays off the hands that you actually make. Take advantage of value bets—it's often worth betting a hand like second or third pair on the river against an opponent capable of calling you with something worse.

Type of Player	Battle Cry	Characteristics	Counter-strategy
The Rock	None. Rocks don't talk.	Supertight before the flop; if he's still betting after the flop, he almost certainly has the goods.	Understand that he's playing a small range of hands—don't reraise with medium hands (small pairs, A-Q) because he'll probably be strong enough to raise you all-in. If he doesn't flop to his hand, however, he's usually looking for a reason to fold. Help him out by bluffing frequently. (You can even *call* a few of his pre-flop raises from position with the intention of bluffing him if he fails to bet the flop.) Attack his blinds before the flop.
The Novice	"How much is it?"	Seems to be fumbling in the dark. Unfamiliar with basic poker etiquette or strategy.	Novices tend to be either too loose or too tight. Figure out which kind you're playing against, and adopt the opposite strategy.
The Pro	"Raise it up!"	Plays smart, tight, aggressive poker. Knows the odds. Is both fearsome and fearless.	There's no shame in avoiding confrontations with a great player—there are usually plenty of other people to pick on. The fact that he's paying close attention can sometimes be exploited if you can figure out how he perceives your table image, but beware of mixing it up with anything less than a strong hand.

Truth be told, tells aren't nearly as important as the movies would lead you to believe. You're rarely, if ever, going to find yourself playing against someone who blinks twice when they have a hand. Some of the more tried-and-true tells—like "strong means weak, weak means strong"— are so well known that even rookie players manage to avoid them.

I'm often asked whether Internet poker is more difficult than live poker because online no one has a physical tell.

Possibly.

But not so much that I'm ever going to worry about it. Physical tells are, by and large, overrated. Most of the really useful tells are behavioral.

What do I mean by behavioral? Most players are creatures of habit. Some feel compelled to toss in a raise any time they flop four cards to a flush. A player who loves to slowplay big hands is often doing that when he just "flat calls" your big bet on the flop. This kind of habitual behavior can be catalogued and exploited whether you're heads-up at a final table on the World Poker Tour or playing an online $2/$4 cash game. Keep an eye out for these patterns in your opponents—and in your own play.

That said, there are a few "physical" tells that translate into—or are even unique to—the online world.

> ### Most of the best tells are behavioral, not physical.

THE FAKE WAIT

In this online variation of the "strong=weak, weak=strong" tell, an opponent who waits, waits, waits, then raises almost always has a very strong hand.

THE QUICK CALL

An opponent who responds to your strong bet or raise with a super-quick, seemingly automatic call is often on a flush or straight draw. Calling with anything else usually comes after a bit of (real or faked) consideration.

THE "DECEPTIVE" SCREEN NAME

See the discussion on Choosing a Screen Name in Chapter One.

THE SUPER-BIG (OR SUPER-SMALL) BUY-IN

Players who buy into a game with what seems like their entire bank-roll aren't often in a state of mind where they are making cool, rational decisions—they're usually being driven by ego or on tilt, or both. Players who buy into a game for the absolute minimum are generally hoping to make a quick score and are on the lookout for a spot to double up in a hurry.

Same Hands Differently, or Different Hands the Same?

It's a deceptively simple question with a remarkably powerful answer: Should I play the same hands differently or play different hands the same way? Is it better, for example, to mix up the way I play pocket aces before the flop—raising different amounts, occasionally limping in with them—or am I better off playing a variety of hands the way I play pocket aces—with a strong pre-flop raise?

Both angles have their merits, and there are probably situations where one works better than the other. On the whole, though, I think it's better to play different hands the same.

In an ideal world, every bet I made would win a pot. We don't live in that kind of world. Bets get called and raised. The trick is to analyze those responses and, hopefully, find meaning in them.

If I raise the same amount with pocket aces every time, then an observant opponent facing that raise will at least have to consider the possibility that I have aces, regardless of whether or not I actually do. If he calls or raises me, I can be pretty sure of one of two things: 1) He thinks I am bluffing, or 2) he has a very strong hand that he believes will beat mine.

Now consider the opposite tactic—mixing up the way I play aces. Sure, I may manage to blindside my opponent every once in a while, but what am I to make of his calls or raises? If he can't make an educated guess as to what I have, then his responses aren't going to provide me with much useful information.

Aggression, Good Misses, and Creating Your Own Luck

Like too many other professional poker players, my primary form of exercise comes from playing golf. Putting aside any argument over the physical benefits (or lack thereof) of smacking a ball around for five hours, you can make an argument that golf can improve your mental preparation at the poker table.

> **While it's good to be unpredictable at the poker table, it's far better to be misunderstood.**

There's a concept in golf called the "good miss." The idea is that some flubs are going to leave you in a better position to recover than others. It's better, for example, to leave a missed putt on the high side of the green than the short side. Or to hit the ball 250 yards onto the fairway instead of 350 yards into the rough.

If you've seen footage of the 2005 World Series of Poker championship event, then you are familiar with Steve Dannenmann. I hadn't—and therefore wasn't—when I first met Steve at an event at the Taj Mahal in Atlantic City. I was surprised to discover not only that I really liked him but that this guy who had been playing serious tournament poker for maybe three months had something valuable to teach me about the game.

It's almost impossible to judge a poker player by his or her appearance, but let's put it this way: If you put out a casting call for someone to portray a great poker player, and Steve showed up, you'd fire the casting director. He's way too polite, much too happy-go-lucky, and— as he'll readily confess—isn't that good at poker. You'd be much more likely to think that the smiling, self-deprecating guy in his 40s was an accountant ... and you'd be right.

But as I sat at the table with Steve, who reluctantly admitted to finishing in second place at the World Series, I was forced to make a reluctant admission of my own: He must be doing something right. I began to interrogate him at every opportunity, looking for clues to his success.

It didn't take long for two of Steve's characteristics to leap out at me. First, he was completely relaxed. By constantly lowering expectations—both of himself, and those of his opponents—he was able to play without any fear. Every action he took seemed to say, "I'm just lucky to be here," or, "It's pretty much impossible for me to make a fool out of myself since I already think I'm a fool."

The second characteristic—and the one I think will ensure that you'll see Steve at many more final tables—is that he always seemed to make a good miss. And in poker, the good miss almost always involves too much aggressiveness.

If you're going to make a mistake at the poker table, it's almost always better to be too aggressive than to be too passive.

Steve may have made a lot of mistakes, but nearly all of them involved too much aggression. His mild-mannered demeanor seemed to be an invitation for opponents to run over him. His lack of fear or ego, however, allowed him to respond to their aggression with even more of his own. "What the heck," he'd say after their raises. "I shouldn't be here anyway. I'm all-in."

Smart? Maybe not. But definitely not not-smart. When you act passively at the poker table—checking when you might bet, calling when you ought to raise—you are hoping for good things to happen to you. Maybe you'll hit that lucky card or, more important, your opponent won't hit his.

When you act aggressively, however, you frquently wind up creating your own luck. Your opponent may fold. Maybe he was bluffing. Even if he turns out to have you beat, there are very few hands that are stone-cold locks to win a heads-up showdown. The chance that an aggressive play will win the hand often compensates for the negative consequences of misreading an opponent's hand. Plus, by actively getting more chips into the middle, you're increasing the amount of money you stand to make should your "mistake" turn into an unexpected victory.

To better explain that last concept, I'll use another sports analogy: the

> ## Playing passively forces you to catch cards to win. Playing aggressively allows you to create your own luck.

onside kick in football. Why do teams bother attempting a play that has only about a 24 percent chance of success? Because the team that tries it is usually in a situation where the best possible end result—recovering possession of the ball without having to play defense—outweighs the (far more likely) negative consequences: Their opponents wind up with the ball *and* great field position. It's better to be a 3–1 underdog with a chance of winning the game than to return the ball to the other team without a fight. And it's sometimes better to be a 3–1 underdog with a chance to win a huge pot than to sacrifice a pot to your opponent that leaves you in a position where it's almost impossible to win a tournament.

Finally, don't forget about the Poker Gods, who are often inspired to perform miracles for their most aggressive believers.

Okay, that last part is more of a superstition. But, as I'm about to argue, it's not necessarily unlucky (or unwise) to be superstitious.

Superstitions

It's unlucky, as the old joke goes, to be superstitious.

My experiences at the poker table, however, have led me to a different conclusion. While I think it's unlucky—or at least unhelpful—to harbor bad superstitions, I think it's great to have positive superstitions.

Do I really believe that wearing a blue sock on my left foot or having an orange lighter in my pocket will make me luckier at the tables? Of course not. But I have found that those little superstitions can occasionally keep me walking in the right direction: feeling good about myself and thinking positively.

Good superstitions have less to do with magic than with ritual and routine. If I always tie my shoe a certain way before a tournament, then I am, consciously or unconsciously, programming my brain, returning to the positive mind-set that has helped me in the past.

The hard part is never associating a superstition with bad luck. I mean, be realistic: Superstitions don't really work ... right?

Bad Beats

"You're not going to believe the bad beat I just took ..."

> **Positive superstitions are rituals that help put you in a winning frame of mind.**

Yes, I will. Believe me. I've taken them all, most of them more than once. Poker is, in the long-term, a game of skill, but it's full of short-term luck. And while bad luck comes in different flavors—flopping a big hand against someone who's flopped a bigger hand, or a seemingly endless runs of terrible starting hands—the most infuriating form is without argument the bad beat.

Bad beats are so annoying that they even have their own special narrative, the "bad beat story."

"Some donkey pushed all-in with bottom pair, then made a runner-runner flush to crack my set ..."

"The idiot called my raise with Q-3, called my bet on the flop—which missed him completely—then caught two running 3s to beat my aces ..."

"He looked up at the sky, yelled, 'Gimme a deuce!' and, sure enough, a deuce on the river ... a two-outer!"

If you've played more than 10 minutes of poker, you're familiar with some (or all) of these stories. Bad beats aren't just inevitable; they're part of the fabric of the game. The key, therefore, is not to avoid them but to avoid letting them throw you off your A-game. Here are a few observations that may help you let them go:

BETTER PLAYERS TAKE MORE BAD BEATS

I once heard a story about Johnny Moss, maybe the greatest poker player of all time, grumbling to his wife about a bad beat he'd just taken. "I don't understand why you're always talking about the bad beats you're taking," she supposedly replied. "Why don't you bad-beat them back?"

Johnny stared at her and said, "Because I don't put my money into the middle when I've got the worst of it."

In order to take a bad beat, you have to have lured your opponent into risking his money on a situation where he was a big underdog. In other words, you have to have done something smart. The smarter you are, the more unfavorable situations you will create for your opponents. When you're playing really well, virtually *all* of your beats will be bad ones.

YOU ARE GOING TO TAKE MORE BAD BEATS ONLINE

It's not because the sites are rigged to "juice" the pots or because your opponents have somehow cracked the system and know which cards are coming, but because you are going to be playing more hands in a shorter period of time. Take a bad beat in a casino and you've at least got a minute or two to calm down as the dealer gathers the cards, scrambles and shuffles, and deals a new hand. When you're multi-tabling online, there's another hand calling for your attention before the bad beat even has a chance to register.

This blazing speed can be a good and a bad thing. On the plus side, you literally do not have time to dwell on a bad beat. There's another hand, hopefully a happier one, waiting for you. The negative is that there's no time to process the bad beat, accept it, and move on. From what (little) I know about psychology, holding feelings like that inside isn't such a good thing. You are eventually going to explode.

There's nothing wrong with taking a breather after a bad beat. Take a walk, smoke a cigarette, punch a wall, or do whatever it is that you have to do to return your heart rate to a normal level and your emotional state to an even keel.

THE BEST WAY TO HANDLE BAD BEATS IS TO TAKE MORE BAD BEATS

I wish I could say I always took bad beats with a reasonable sense of calm, but over the years I have left a trail of pulverized mice (of the computer variety) that tell a different story.

Not so much anymore. Yes, the beats still hurt. But after you've taken the same bad beat a thousand times or so, it feels less like the end of the world than a momentary feeling of mild annoyance.

MOST BAD BEATS AREN'T NEARLY AS BAD AS YOU THINK

Let's begin at the beginning: No starting hand in poker is unbeatable, and most are more vulnerable than you think. Pocket aces beat a smaller pair four out of five times in heads-up confrontations. Ace-king beats 7-2 offsuit only two out of three times. You are *supposed* to lose a good portion of those confrontations—that's what makes poker poker.

Another thing to keep in mind is that large pots often make it correct for players to chase all kinds of hands. A player who hangs around a multi-way pot with bottom pair, then *backdoors* his way into a flush or a straight may, in fact, be getting the right odds to do so. (If you're unfamiliar with the concept of pot odds, check out the appendices.)

By getting angry over a bad beat, you may wind up giving an opponent the correct implied odds to draw out on you. He probably wasn't getting the right odds to call your bet on the flop with middle pair when you clearly had an overpair to the board. But when he nails a second pair on the turn and check-raises you (a bet you angrily call), then bets again on the river—leading to another angry call from you—he may wind up creating a pot big enough to make his initial decision to call on the flop look like a good one.

YOU WANT PLAYERS TO PLAY BADLY AGAINST YOU

While your temptation may be to ask the deliverer of a bad beat just how he could be such a huge jackass, you already know the answer: because you want him to be. You want people to call your bets when they have the worst of it. If they don't, the only way you can ever make money playing poker would be to bluff or to catch luckier cards than the next guy.

The Bad Player Paradox

If there were no bad beats and the good players always fleeced the bad, then it wouldn't take long for the bad players to run out of money. No more money, no more action. Bad beats are a necessary evil in the poker economy, as they give bad players hope that, on any given day, any two cards can win. Keep that in mind the next time you're ready to throttle somebody!

YOU WILL (OCCASIONALLY) BAD BEAT OTHER PEOPLE

I don't care who you are. There will be times when you will be just as guilty as the game's biggest donkeys of lucking out in a situation where you have the worst of it.

Most Hold'em players refer to a starting hand of 10-2 as a Doyle Brunson, an homage to the great player who used that starting hand to win back-to-back World Series championships. What they usually don't remember is that the first time around, Brunson had to catch two running cards on the turn and the river to make a full house against his opponent, who had flopped top two pair. The following year, Doyle won when he made second pair with a deuce on the turn to eliminate a guy who had flopped bottom two pair.

There's not a sane person in the world who would describe Doyle as a bad poker player, and in his defense, he had his opponent out-chipped in both cases, giving him room to gamble.* But a big part of the reason everyone has heard of Texas Dolly—while few people talk about Jessie Alto or "Bones" Berland (his two victims)—is that Doyle

---

*To be fair to Doyle, in the second case, his opponent actually checked the flop, hoping to slow-play the hand, allowing Doyle a free look at the winning card.

got luckier than his opponents, delivering what many people would describe as bad beats.

You'll never—or, at least, you shouldn't—deliver more bad beats than you take. You'd be a horrible poker player if you did. But you will occasionally win a pot you shouldn't. When you do, take a minute to acknowledge the shifting sands of chance, and try to store the memory somewhere you can find it the next time someone draws out against you.

THERE'S NOTHING GOOD ABOUT A BAD BEAT STORY

I don't know what it is about the human condition that seems to force people who have suffered bad beats to talk about them to anyone who will listen. What I do know is that it doesn't help. Yes, your audience may be nodding politely while offering generic condolences, but they do not really care. Even worse, by retelling the story, you are perpetuating negative emotions that may prevent you from playing your best poker.

The New Player's Axis of Evil: Bluffing, Check-Raising, and Slowplaying

Sometime during the late 1960s, basketball players discovered the slam dunk. It didn't take long to catch on—why earn two points with an easy layup when you can electrify the crowd by jamming it down over a hapless opponent?

Along with the dunk came an equally memorable image: the missed dunk. A player steals the ball, drives down the court, leaps into the air ... and clangs the ball off the back of the rim. An easy two points lost in the service of style.

A lot of poker is making the easy layup. You wait for a good hand in a good spot, bet or raise when it's your turn, and take down a small pot. For many players—especially new ones—the routine quickly becomes numbing. What about bluffing? Or springing a trap on an opponent with a surprise raise on the river? Poker is supposed to be exciting, isn't it?

Well, yes ... sometimes. But just like in basketball, you don't get extra points for style. And in poker, it's even easier to clang the ball off the back of the rim.

Bluffing

Imagine a world where everyone was a solid poker player, making the "correct" move in every situation. The game would essentially be a card-catching contest, like bingo. The only way for one player, over the long haul, to outplay the competition would be to bluff.

Bluffing is obviously a big part of the game. But the reality is that most poker players don't make the correct move in every situation, making bluffing much less important than you might think. In order for a bluff to be successful, three conditions must be met:

1) Your opponent has to have a better hand than you.

2) You have to be able to represent a hand better than your opponent.

3) Your opponent has to believe—strongly enough to fold—that you have the hand you are representing.

Let's take a closer look at each of these conditions ...

YOUR OPPONENT HAS TO HAVE A BETTER HAND THAN YOU

This may seem obvious, but it's amazing how often players forget this part of the equation. Let's say you raise before the flop with A-K. Everyone folds to the big blind, who calls you. The flop comes Q-6-6, the big blind checks, you bet and win the pot when he folds.

Did you just bluff your opponent? Probably not. Your A-K was almost certainly the best hand, and your continuation *bet* on the flop reminded your opponent. There is nothing fancy about betting with the stronger hand.

YOU HAVE TO BE ABLE TO REPRESENT A HAND BETTER THAN YOUR OPPONENT

A successful bluff works because it preys on your opponent's worst fears. Like ghost stories, environment is everything. A tale about a psycho killer with a hook for a hand isn't going to freak anybody out if you tell it over tea and crumpets at a garden party. Tell the same story on a dark night in the middle of the woods, however, and you just might get your audience to scream.

In poker, your environment is the board. Calling a tight player's raise, then bluffing into a 7-2-2 flop isn't going to work very often— he's probably not going to believe that you have a 7 or a 2. You want a board full of cobwebs and dark corners: possible straights and flushes, or paired cards that seem likely to match something in your hand.

YOUR OPPONENT HAS TO BELIEVE—STRONGLY ENOUGH TO FOLD— THAT YOU HAVE THE HAND YOU ARE REPRESENTING

This is the biggest reason *not* to bluff when you are playing against weak players—many of them won't be paying close enough attention to absorb the story that you're trying to tell, and even if they are, they may not have the discipline required to make the "good" laydown. This is the great paradox of bluffs: They work best against smart players.

The worse the player, the harder it is to bluff him.

The "strongly enough to fold" part is also critical here. In a limit game, it's often worthwhile for a player to (literally) call your bluff. If there are 10 big bets in the pot when you decide to bet on the river, a player almost has to call you if he thinks there's even a small chance you are bluffing—he has to be right less than 10 percent of the time for his call to be a profitable play. The same thinking applies to no-limit tournaments, where it's tough to bluff a very small or a very big stack—neither of their prospects are likely to change very much by calling.

You may have already figured out that the opposite thinking is true as well—you don't have to be successful every time for bluffing to be a profitable play. There's even some benefit to getting caught in a bluff from time to time, as you may wind up making a little more money from your skeptical opponents when you actually make a legitimate hand. But keep in mind that there's a significant downside to earning a reputation as a bluffer. Your pre-flop raises will get less respect, resulting in more multi-way pots—and more opportunities to lose. When other players start playing sheriff against you, calling you down to the river just to keep you honest, you put yourself in a position where you actually have to catch cards, making the strongest hand to win. And remember the "same hand differently, different hands the same" argument? Players will call bluffers with a much wider range of hands, making it much more difficult to figure out what your opponents are holding.

Although it may go without saying, I'll say it anyway: It's a lot easier to bluff one or two opponents than it is to steal a multi-way pot. There's just too big a chance that someone has enough of a hand to make a call worthwhile.

You'll make a lot of your early bluff-related income—especially in low-limit games—by picking off other players' bluffs. You'll start to notice the obvious bluffing situations, like a bet on the river after everyone has checked the turn. You want to be the guy calling these bets, not making them.

On a related note, it's usually bad poker to bet or raise on the river with a hand that might win a showdown unless you are relatively sure that your opponent will call you with a worse hand. If he will only call (or raise!) with a hand stronger than yours, you are wasting money. You are better off checking and calling. You'll not only get to see the showdown for the same amount you would have spent on a bet, you'll often induce a bluff from a player who might otherwise have folded.

You're often better off checking your medium-strength hands on the river, especially when your opponent won't call unless he has you beat or you may be able to induce your opponent to bluff at the pot.

The exception to this rule is the value bet, a bet made against an opponent who, say, will call your middle pair with bottom pair or ace high, but these situations don't arise too often. If you decided to never bet the river unless you were absolutely bluffing with a chance to steal the pot, you probably wouldn't cause any significant harm to your bottom line.*

Finally, there's a huge difference between a bluff and a *semi-bluff*, a bet made with a hand that, while not currently in front, has a chance of developing into a winner. A bluff gives you only one way to win—your opponent(s) must fold. A semi-bluff not only gives you additional equity—you have a chance to draw out should you get called—but will occasionally cause your opponents to miss a bet they should have made, buying you a free card on the turn.

---

*This assumes, of course, that your opponents are unaware of your philosophy.

Check-Raising

There's something about this play that appeals to everyone's inherent sneakiness—you feign weakness with a check, give your opponent enough confidence to toss in a bet, and BLAM! You come over the top with a raise. Satisfying, and potentially expensive ... for you!

When you check with the intention of check-raising, one of two things will happen: 1) Your opponent(s) will check behind you, claiming a free card and a chance to draw to a hand better than yours, or 2) an opponent will bet, leading you to spring your trap.

But how profitable is your trap? By check-raising, you are representing a very strong hand to your opponents. If the bettor was bluffing, he'll almost certainly fold, costing you the opportunity to pull extra money out of him should he decide to continue with his bluff. If the bettor has a good-but-not-great hand, he'll probably fold it as well. You'll make the same money you would have had you led with a bet and been called, while losing the chance to make any money from him on later streets. If the bettor had a good enough hand to call a check-raise he might have raised your initial bet, giving you a chance to reraise and make even more money!

Finally, if he was betting with a draw, you may wind up presenting him with even better odds to pursue it. There are now three extra bets in the pot—his original bet and the two you just added with the check-raise—and it will cost him only a single bet to see another card. In some cases, you'll wind up building a pot so big that it's profitable for him to call you all the way to the river with a draw that he would have thrown away had you simply decided to bet on the flop.

I'm not saying that check-raising isn't a powerful tool; I'm just trying to point out that it shouldn't be your default play when you flop a big hand. Simply betting out is usually the most profitable play. There are, however, a few exceptions ...

USE A CHECK-RAISE TO BLUFF

A check-raise sends a simple, unambiguous message—"I am strong!"—which occasionally makes it a great tool for bluffing. Let's say I've got a garbage hand against a single opponent and we check all the way down to the river. I check again, and my opponent finally decides to bet. He's almost certainly bluffing, or at least *thinks* he's bluffing, as his garbage may be more than enough to beat mine. It may be a perfect spot for me to check-raise—I must have been slowplaying a *monster*!

USE A CHECK-RAISE TO TRAP MORE MONEY ON THE FLOP

If I'm in a multi-way pot, with a loose, aggressive player on my left, and I flop a monster, I will often check-raise to trap more money in the pot. The idea is that my check will encourage the player on my left to bet, other players will call him, and I will—hopefully—take an even bigger pot when the action gets back to me and I stick in my raise. This can be a risky play, however, as the extra money that gets added can create a pot so juicy that it becomes worthwhile for opponents to call me with all kinds of draws. Use it with caution!

USE A CHECK-RAISE TO NARROW THE FIELD

When you have an aggressive player to your immediate right who everyone knows will bet almost every time it gets checked around to him, it's sometimes good to give him the chance. He bets, you raise, and everyone else in the hand is suddenly confronted with a double bet, making it much less profitable to hang around with a drawing hand. The nice thing about this play is that you can pull it off even if you don't have a hand. No one is going to call or raise you unless they have a powerhouse—in which case you can gracefully fold at first opportunity—and your show of "strength" will often be enough to persuade the aggressive player (who was probably bluffing anyway) to throw his hand away.

Slowplaying

Almost every player loves to slowplay when they start playing poker. Nearly every good player learns to hate it.

I remember the day the lightbulb went off for me. I was deep into a tournament when a player with a big stack opened with a raise from early position. I looked down to find pocket aces—hooray!—and reraised. Everyone folded to the initial raiser, who called my bet.

The flop came 4-4-2, and the initial raiser bet into me. Since it was incredibly unlikely that he would have called a pre-flop raise out of position with any hand that had me beat, I was pretty sure he had an overpair. Figuring that there were only two cards left in the deck that could beat me, I decided to get sneaky, calling his bet with the intention of raising on the turn.

The turn was another ace, giving me a nearly unbeatable full house. Good for me? Of course not! He immediately shut down. I bet, he folded, and my opportunity to milk any more money out of what could have been a dream situation—a chance to double up late in a tournament—came to a crashing halt.

As I grumbled to myself over my "bad luck," I began to realize there were a lot of cards that I didn't want to see on the turn. Any picture card would either improve his hand (if he was holding something like jacks or queens) or increase his fear that I was holding a bigger hand. A similar argument could even be made for some middle cards. In fact, the only cards that would have helped my cause would have been low cards—fewer than half of the cards remaining in the deck.

I realized I would have been much better off raising his bet on the flop, putting him to a decision. At worst, he would have folded, earning me exactly the same amount that I wound up winning. In truth, however, it would have been very difficult for him to fold an overpair to the board. He may very well have wound up calling, even reraising my bet. Not only did I let him off the hook, I did so in a way that almost certainly triggered his suspicions: What hand could I possibly have that was good enough to reraise with before the flop but only worth a call after a flop as nonthreatening as this one?

Therein lies the rub: The real problem with slowplaying isn't that you'll give an opponent a chance to draw out on you (although this is a very real danger), but that there usually plenty of cards left in the deck that, should they appear, will slow down the action on later streets.

You are decreasing the chances that your opponent will make a big mistake. A lot of players who will call a bet or raise on the flop with a flush draw will shut down when they fail to get there on the turn. An opponent with top pair might go four bets on the flop, but good luck getting the same kind of action out of him on the river!

Slowplaying doesn't just give your opponents a free or cheap shot at chasing a draw but may also save them from making bigger and costlier mistakes.

The only time I really advocate slowplaying is against big-time opponents in big-time tournaments—trapping a top pro is usually the only way you are going to get him to lose a substantial number of chips. But even this shouldn't be automatic. When you've got the deck crippled—holding K-10, for example, when the flop comes K-10-10—what is the point of slowplaying? I'm just as likely to bet out, hoping my opponent has enough of a hand to pay me off or, better yet, decides that I am bluffing and fires back with a bluff of his own.

Remember that the chances of your opponent's hitting a miracle card—one that will improve his hand without making it better than yours—are just that ... miraculous. You're almost always better off playing in a straightforward manner, leaving the door open for your "tricky" opponents to hang themselves. Even if they manage to escape, you're still the one raking in the chips at the end of the hand.

Putting It All Together: Fear and Folding at the Aussie Millions

One of the interesting aspects of playing online is that you wind up developing friendships with—or at least mutual admiration for—a whole bunch of people you may never get the chance to meet in real life. It's cool when you actually do get to meet one of these people face-to-face, as I did when I finally met Richard, a New Zealander I'd frequently run into online, at a poker tournament in Australia. What was even more impressive was watching him play a hand that managed to embody almost every concept covered in this chapter.

It was the first day of the tournament, and Richard found himself heads-up in an unraised pot holding J-10. His opponent—let's call him Ace—held A-4 but decided to check the A-5-2 flop. Richard bluffed at the pot, hoping to represent an ace of his own, but Ace quickly called.

The turn card was a 4. Ace, who had about $2,500 in chips, led out with a $500 bet. The obvious thing for Richard to do would have been to fold. Instead, he raised to $1,200. He didn't believe that Ace held a 3 (making a straight) and wanted to reinforce the message that he'd been sending with his bluff on the flop: "I'm the one holding an ace, Ace!"

Richard had, of course, miscalculated, as his opponent had two pair, a hand that could beat an ace. But his mistake was an aggressive mistake—the "correct" mistake—and put him in a position to create his own luck.

What was Ace to make of the raise? Exactly what Richard wanted him to believe: that Richard was holding an ace with a strong kicker. Instead of reraising, however, Ace decided to slowplay the hand, taking the passive course of action. He called.

When the river paired the 5 on the board, you could almost hear Ace groan out loud. His two pair had been *counterfeited*, giving both men aces and 5s, and Richard *had* to have a bigger kicker. Ace checked, Richard bet, and Ace folded, turning over his cards to show everyone just how unlucky he was. Richard raked in a big pot.

Keep in mind that Richard was never at any point ahead in this hand. But he played it aggressively, betting or raising at every opportunity, represented a hand his opponent would believe, and took advantage of the lucky river card. Ace, who was in fact ahead throughout the entire hand, played passively, checking on every street except the turn (where he allowed Richard to regain the upper hand with a raise), failed to take down the pot when he suspected he had the best hand, and found himself stuck in a position where luck could only work against him.

No Regrets

Some days you are going to play like Richard. Other days you may feel like Ace. The most important thing—and I can't stress this enough—is to remember that every session, every tournament, every hand is an opportunity for you to make good things happen.

When I make a bad play, especially one that gets me knocked out of a tournament, the first words that usually spring into my head are, "God, am I an idiot."

The feeling never lasts more than a second or two. I remember that poker is a game of decisions. Each time I was confronted with a decision, I took my time, analyzed the Factors, and came up with a course of action. Whether it was a good decision that just didn't pan out for me or an altogether terrible decision, at least I know I had some reason for doing what I did.

Everybody at the table might think that my decision sucked. Someone might even post the hand history online, showing the entire world (or at least that narrow subset who read poker blogs) what an idiotic decision I made. But as long as I remember that I had a reason for doing what I did, I'll never have any regrets.

It's good practice to question the Factors you use to make a decision, but as long as you're taking the time to think through each play, there's no point in beating yourself up over the decisions you make.

Darrell "Gigabet" Dicken

What can I say about Gigabet? He's already a rock star in the online poker world, and now, having earned a grueling win at the WSOP circuit event at Rincon, he's a superstar in the brick-and-mortar world as well!

I can't tell you how fortunate I was to meet him when I did. Gigabet played a huge role in helping me develop my poker mind-set, not to mention my professional poker career. He has taught

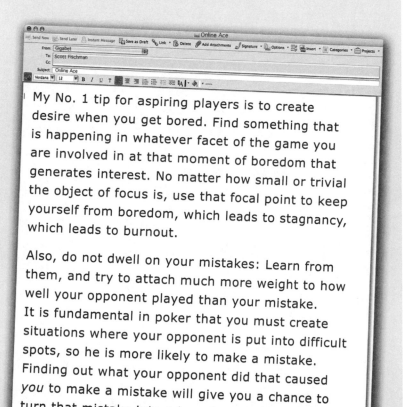

My No. 1 tip for aspiring players is to create desire when you get bored. Find something that is happening in whatever facet of the game you are involved in at that moment of boredom that generates interest. No matter how small or trivial the object of focus is, use that focal point to keep yourself from boredom, which leads to stagnancy, which leads to burnout.

Also, do not dwell on your mistakes: Learn from them, and try to attach much more weight to how well your opponent played than your mistake. It is fundamental in poker that you must create situations where your opponent is put into difficult spots, so he is more likely to make a mistake. Finding out what your opponent did that caused *you* to make a mistake will give you a chance to turn that mistake into a learning experience, one that you probably can use directly against future opponents who have a skill level similar to yours.

Darrell "Gigabet" Dicken

me more about myself than any other single person, helping me to elevate my game to the next level.

I don't think there is a living player, online or otherwise, who has put more deep thought into the game than Gigabet has. His dedication to poker is absolutely incredible.

CHAPTER SIX:
Multi-Table Tournaments

SIT-N-GOs AND CASH GAMES can be a lot of fun and a great way to build a bankroll online, but they're not going to get you rich unless you're playing at the upper limits. And you shouldn't be playing the upper limits unless you've got the bankroll, i.e., you're *already* rich.

If you're looking for a faster score, you're going to have to start playing in multi-table tournaments. They represent a much bigger risk than cash games or Sit-N-Gos—generally only 10 percent or so of the field will make the money—but the payoffs can be absolutely enormous. In the 2005 World Series championship, each of the players at the final table received at least $1 million. The winner, Joseph Hachem, earned $7.5 million, the highest payout in poker history. I wouldn't bet against it being even higher this year.

You used to have to wait until the World Series came around to play in a big-money tournament. Now there seems to be a $10,000 buy-in event every other week. The action online is no less lucrative—there are plenty of big events with six- and seven-figure prize pools taking place on a weekly basis. The $215 entry no-limit Hold'em tournament held each Sunday at PokerStars features a guaranteed prize pool of at least $750,000.

You don't have to win a huge one for the money to be life altering. Going into 2004, I had enjoyed a few successes in the $2,000 to $3,000 range. I managed to kick off the year with a fourth-place finish in the Grand American Classic—good for more than $6,464—and it just got better from there. I won more than $400,000 at the World Series, won a series of $40,000 prizes toward the end of the summer, and ended the year with a $70,000 second-place finish in an event at the Five Diamond Classic. After all was said and done, I earned nearly $700,000 at multi-table tournaments in 2004. Not bad for a kid who a year earlier was pitching the cards and just a couple of years before that might have been the guy parking your car!

There's no reason you can't do the same thing.

Satellites

At first glance, the big tournaments may seem way out of your reach. It costs $10,000 to enter the World Series championship event, and odds are, you don't have that kind of money to spend on something as speculative as a poker tournament. Fortunately, there are *satellites*—preliminary tournaments with a fraction of the entry fee that can earn you a ticket to a much bigger event.

Who uses satellites? Everybody. While there aren't any official records to confirm it, it's pretty safe to say that based on the claims from virtual cardrooms, around 60 percent of the 5,619 players in last year's WSOP championship won their way in through some kind of lower-priced online satellite. (That's not including the hundreds of people who won their way in playing live satellites.)

There are satellites for every budget, from single-table "freeze-outs" (which cost about one-tenth of the event's entry fee) to $1 supersatellites (tournaments that win you spots in more expensive satellites). If having to win a supersatellite to make a satellite to cash in a big event sounds like an unlikely path, you need only look to the story of a PokerStars player called Money800 who accomplished exactly that in 2003. You probably know him by his real name: Chris Moneymaker. Moneymaker, as most know, parlayed a $39 online supersatellite into a $2.5 million victory at the 2003 World Series of Poker.

Winning these kinds of tournaments involves a pretty similar strategy to the one you've been using to (hopefully) crush Sit-N-Gos, but with a couple of slight alterations.

One-Table Satellites

I love one-table satellites. If you're an average or above-average player—that is, as good or better than half the players you're competing against—and you're thinking about entering a $100 buy-in tournament, why not enter ten $10 satellites instead? Odds are pretty good you'll win one before you hit the 10th, earning you at least a modest discount on the price.

> **The best thing about satellites is that they offer you a chance to play above the limits of your bankroll.**

Let's say you've been grinding it out at the tables to build $2,000 in poker capital. You're not going to risk half of that to play in a $1,000 buy-in tournament. But it's certainly reasonable to play in a few $100 one-table satellites for the same event, giving you a great opportunity to shoot for the moon.

If you think these events look a lot like Sit-N-Gos, you're right. The only major strategic difference is that there's no reward for second or third place. You are going to need *all* the chips at the end in order to win. And I think that to give yourself the best shot at gathering all the chips, you need to play a little looser in the early part of the tournament.

The key is not to get carried away—I'm not advocating that you play a lot of junk hands like the pros seem to do on TV. I'm talking about little things. Maybe you'll limp in to a multi-way pot with 7-6 suited or call a moderate raise with K-Q suited. The idea is to take a few more small risks early in the hopes of flopping a powerful hand or a great draw (like an open-ended straight flush) that you can move all-in with in the hopes of doubling up.

Multi-Table Satellites

There's an expression in poker: "Tight is right." In no case is this truer than in a multi-table satellite.

You usually don't have to win a multi-table satellite to reap the benefits. At the start of the tournament, once all the entry money has been added up, the host will announce how many seats will be given away to whichever bigger tournament you're playing for.

The goal is not to win the tournament, or even to gather a lot of chips, but to survive long enough to win one of these seats. As long as you have enough chips to cover the blinds and antes, there's no reason to take that many chances with your stack.

I'm occasionally asked if I will ever fold pocket aces before the flop. My answer is yes—in multi-table satellites. If there are 11 players fighting it out for 10 spots and I've got even an average-size stack, pocket aces is the last hand I need to see. If someone with more chips than I have pushes all-in before the flop, I'll pretend I was dealt two blank pieces of paper, or that I was in the bathroom, or anything else I can think of to trick my mind into folding the hand. Why risk all of my money in a situation where I have an 80 percent chance of winning—in other words, a 20 percent chance of losing!—when there's probably close to a 100 percent chance that someone else will bust out in the next two or three orbits around the table?

As long as you have enough chips to reach your goal, you don't need confrontation. I know a lot of players who dominate multi-table satellites, sometimes winning several seats in the same tournament (which they later turn around and sell to less-fortunate players). The players who win six or seven tickets to WPT Aruba are willing to throw away aces at the final table, happily waiting for one of the players who push all-in with A-K to suffer the inevitable bad beat.

In multi-table satellites where more than one seat is given away, it is much more important to preserve your stack than to take significant risks trying to increase it.

Multi-Table Tournaments

My pregame strategy for multi-table tournaments looks a lot like what I do for Sit-N-Gos. There are three seasons (beginning, middle, end) and three basic strategies for each (tight play, picking spots, aggressive stack-pushing). I'll examine the structure of the tournament—looking at the number of chips I'll start with in relation to the size of the blinds and the rate at which they increase—and try to figure out when each season is likely to change.

Unlike with Sit-N-Gos—which condense a lot of action into a short period of time—the structure of multi-table tournaments can vary wildly from one to the next. In the World Series of Poker championship, players start with $10,000 in chips and $25/$50 blinds, which are increased every two hours. The large number of chips compared with the blinds—you've got enough to cover 150 orbits—and the long levels mean that you can afford to play patiently and selectively. You've got a lot of time before you reach the middle stages.

At the other extreme, there are online tournaments where you'll start with 30 big blinds and face increases every 10 or 15 minutes. You're going to have to start making moves with less-than-premium hands almost immediately.

Many multi-table tournaments also have *antes* that kick in during the later stages. Antes not only increase the "price" you'll have to pay during each orbit—forcing you to make critical decisions earlier in the tournament—but also increase the amount of money sitting in the middle before the flop, making it even more worthwhile to steal the pot with a pre-flop raise.

> **It's a good idea to take a beforehand look at the blind structure of any tournament you intend to play. While your strategy will obviously change once you're in the thick of it, it's good to go in with a sense of when you want to think about changing gears.**

Another pregame Factor to consider is the prize structure. Multi-table tournaments usually pay prizes to a percentage of finishers relative to the number of people who enter. The idea of the bubble—the line that separates the money winners from the also-rans—becomes even more critical. You will often have to decide late in a tournament between preserving your stack in the hopes of squeezing into the money or making riskier moves to gather enough chips to give you a better shot at first prize. More important, your opponents will be making the same decision, significantly affecting the way you decide to play at them during this critical stage of the tournament.

Another consideration is the "flatness" of the prize structure. Some tournaments are top-heavy in the way they pay out, reserving most of the prize money for the very last finishers. Others are flatter, distributing the cash more evenly among all the players who finish in the money. This, too, will figure into any decision about whether to play conservatively or aggressively as you approach the bubble. (I've included sample blind structures in the appendices.)

Finally, you are going to want to consider how many people have entered the tournament. A 40-person event with a relaxed blind structure may not be worth your time if your goal is to maximize profits: It will take a long time to compete for a pot of gold that, thanks to the small number of entry fees, won't be that golden.

Rebuys and Add-Ons

Players love tournaments because they allow them to risk a relatively small amount to win a lot more. Tournament organizers do their part by looking for ways to increase the size of their prize pools.

Rebuys offer players who have busted out of a tournament during its early stages—usually the first hour or so—the chance to buy back in. Add-ons allow each player the chance to spend real-world money to buy extra tournament chips at specific moments in the event, usually at the beginning of the first break in the action.

Lots of players hate these kinds of tournaments. The ability to replenish one's chips leads to all kinds of loose play during the add-on/rebuy period as players look to gamble in the hopes of building an enormous stack. There are also people who love rebuy tournaments, believing that the structure increases their potential equity without costing them any more money. Their thinking, more or less, is that the bad players—who don't have much chance of winning anyway—will wind up spending a lot on rebuys, essentially subsidizing the good players who have a chance of winning.

For me, the truth lies somewhere in between: I believe that rebuys and add-ons *do* increase my equity, but I also believe that "gambling it up" in the first hour can be a great way to improve my overall prospects. I am prepared, therefore, to spend my money to buy nearly every chip that is available to me.

Are there ever times when I would consider not rebuying or adding on? Sure, but it's never a bankroll decision. In other words, I go into each of these tournaments assuming I am going to have to shell out for an add-on and at least one rebuy. If I don't have the bankroll to buy more chips as needed, then I am playing in the wrong tournament.

> **The decision to rebuy or add on should be motivated by the size and structure of the tournament. If your bankroll is a consideration, you're playing in the wrong tournament.**

In order for an add-on to be worthwhile, it has to cover a few extra blinds and antes, buying me more time to wait for a good spot or add enough chips to allow me to survive losing an extra hand. Whether I choose to do it is determined more by the blind structure than the size of my stack—if the add-on buys me only four or five big blinds and I already have plenty of chips, I might pass, but any more than that and I will almost definitely buy as many add-ons as I can.

Rebuys are an easier decision: You either need them or you don't. The real question is whether I am going to alter my early strategy—

playing looser and gambling more—to take advantage of my ability to buy back my chips should I lose. The answer here depends on the size and structure of the tournament. If it's a huge field or a large, guaranteed prize pool, I will gamble like a madman during the rebuy period. Change that to a small field without a guaranteed prize pool, and it might not be worth investing the extra cash—I'll stick with the same old conservative strategy I'd use in a tournament without rebuys.

One last Factor to consider before plotting your rebuy strategy: Take a look at how tables get broken down. Every tournament has a method for shuffling around the survivors when enough players have been eliminated. Some sites break down the table where the last player was eliminated (moving all the remaining players into empty seats at new tables), while others break them down in order, starting, for example, with Table No. 100, then No. 99, No. 98, etc., until only one table remains.

Why does this matter? Because if I'm at a table that I know will be among the first to get broken down, I won't play like a rebuying madman. If I have to rebuy, I want to have the chance to win back the chips I have lost. I can't do that if the players I've been kind enough to "loan" my chips to are suddenly scattered throughout the tournament. There's nothing worse than rebuying 10 times, having your table broken down, then finding yourself at a new table where *no one* has purchased a rebuy. I don't like contributing money to the poker economy without the possibility of recouping my investment.

> **Before you rebuy in a tournament, make sure you're going to have a chance to win back the money you've already lost.**

So before you yell, "Any two will do!" and start gambling like crazy, check the site rules (or talk to the tournament director) to see how tables get broken down.

The Tournament Lobby

Another difference between Sit-N-Gos and multi-table tournaments: You can't choose your lucky seat. Click on a tournament and you'll usually find yourself in a lobby specific to the event. There is a tremendous amount of information here, much more than you have available to you in a brick-and-mortar tournament setting.

When it comes to the size of your stack in a tournament, you already know that its absolute value is less important than its relative value to the blinds and antes. In multi-table tournaments—especially no-limit and pot-limit tournaments—you've also got to account for your stack's size relative to everyone else's. You may have plenty of chips to cover the blinds, but if most of your opponents have a lot more money than you, it's a lot easier for them to push you around, forcing you to make decisions for all your chips.

In a brick-and-mortar event, obtaining even a rough idea of this information requires you to figure out how much money is in play (multiplying the number of entrants by the entry fee while accounting for any rebuys or add-ons), then stand up, look around the room to estimate how many players are remaining, and divide the total prize pool by the number of survivors.

It's a lot easier in an online tournament: You just click on the lobby. You've got instant access to the exact number of people in the tournament, how many chips are in play, the average stack size, as well as the size of the biggest and shortest stacks. No guesstimating or math required. Most lobbies even allow you to look at each individual table, where you can see how your friends (or sworn enemies) are doing.

The exact payouts are usually available the instant the rebuy/add-on period (if any) is over. You'll also find a tournament clock that will let you know how much time is remaining until the next increase in blinds and antes or the next break.

If there's any problem with the lobby of an online tournament, it's that there's *too* much information. It's easy to get caught up in watching the number of players remaining as it dwindles quickly (or seems like it isn't dwindling at all). Or comparing your stack to the average after every hand. Or engaging in internal debates about the relative merits of different finishes—"Wow ... seventh place pays twice as much as eighth!"—long before you even reach the bubble.

If there's a common theme to my most successful results in larger tournaments, it's been blurriness. That's right—every moment, from the beginning of the tournament up to a point just prior to the bubble, is a big blur. I don't wear a watch. I am able to shut off my mind to the concept of time, never concentrating on how long I've already been sitting or how soon the next break will arrive. I try not to think about how many hundreds of people are remaining; instead, I trick my brain into believing that I'm playing a never-ending one-table tournament. I don't get hung up on my exact chip count: As long as I have a big enough stack to do what I want to do at my table, I won't have to worry too much

> **Online tournaments offer a lot more readily available information than their brick-and-mortar counterparts, but try not to let that distract you— the most important Factors to consider on any hand are those *specific* to that hand: What is the best way to play the cards in front of me?**

about how much I have compared with the rest of the field. On my best days I'm able to reach—and maintain—an almost euphoric state where it's just me, sitting in a room full of empty tables and chairs, playing poker.

In other words, just let it flow! Positive emotions and solid play are much more important than, say, knowing who the chip leader is with 200 players remaining.

The Beginning

I've already told you my strategy for early tournament play: Tight is right. I try to build my stack slowly, always on the lookout for spots to double up without exposing myself to too much risk. But I have to admit I'll tweak this tactic depending on whether I'm in a live or an online setting.

When I travel to a casino for a tournament, I'm looking to win, of course, but I'll also consider my entertainment value—poker's not all work, you know. I'm not likely to go all-in on the first or second hand (or the 20th or 30th hand, for that matter) unless I'm holding the nuts or something close to it. Few things feel worse than making a long trip to get knocked out of a live tournament early on a stupid play.

Online poker is a different story. I'll sometimes play five or six tournaments—at the same time! The question isn't "How will I do in this tournament?" but "How will my bankroll look at the end of the day?" Since it doesn't hurt as much to get eliminated from any one tournament, I'll take a few more risks with my chips at the beginning. For example, if I flop an open-ended straight flush draw in the early stages of an online tournament, I'll almost always push all-in. I might even make the same play with just a flush or a straight draw. (Note that in all these cases, I want to be the guy raising all-in, not calling an all-in raise. It's not just the actual value of the hand that allows me to make the play but also the *fold equity* associated with my raise.)

In online tournaments—especially ones with rapidly increasing blinds—I love to double up early. This isn't true for everyone. I know a lot of extremely good players who would much rather settle in to a tournament, throwing away all but the most premium hands as they take mental notes on their opponents' skills and tendencies, increasing their chances of finding the right spots during the later stages. But for me, doubling up early creates a comfort zone. I can play more hands and take bigger risks. You might want to experiment with both strategies to see which makes you feel more comfortable.

The Middle

My strategy for the middle stages of a multi-table tournament is essentially the same as it is for Sit-N-Gos—picking spots, looking to gradually build my stack. I don't want to get into a showdown unless I have to, but I am definitely guilty of making the occasional all-in move, sometimes even on a bluff, if I feel like there's enough fold equity to make it worthwhile.

There are a couple of additional Factors to consider in a multi-table tournament, namely how you are feeling, who is at your table, and your position in relation to those players.

How you are feeling is more important than you might realize. While a lot of people laugh at the idea of poker being a sport, there's no doubt it requires a surprising amount of endurance. Multi-table tournaments are the marathons of the poker world. They can take a long time to complete—several days, in the case of the bigger ones—and unlike a regular ring game, you can't cash out if you're feeling tired or otherwise off your game.

And in a long tournament, there are plenty of chances to get knocked off your game. Maybe it's a bad beat you shouldn't have taken, a cell phone call you shouldn't have answered, or a huge meal you shouldn't

> Since you'll (hopefully) be locked into a
> multi-table tournament for an extended period
> of time, it's even more critical to remain aware
> of your emotional state, including anger,
> fatigue, and hunger.

have scarfed down. You will inevitably experience moments when your concentration drifts away, or negative ideas start to intrude on your thinking.

Equally important are preventive measures. Try to get enough sleep before playing in a tournament. Turn off your cell phone. Avoid big meals that will leave you drowsy. Most important, don't dwell on the size of your stack. A lot of players, as soon as they hit a 15-minute break, love to count their chips and swap totals with their buddies. But, seriously, with 400 players left in a tournament, does it really matter whether you have $2,200 or $2,700 in chips? When someone asks me how I'm doing, I usually give my stock answer:

"I'm still in!"

The second and third considerations—who is at your table and your relative position to them—are tied together. Ideally, depending on the way the tables break, you'll wind up spending a lot more time with your tablemates in a multi-table tournament, allowing you to gather more information on them than you could in a shorter game. You should know by the middle of the tournament who will defend his blinds and who will throw them away. Who is capable of laying down a big hand? Who likes to slowplay? Who likes to bluff?

With this information at your disposal, you'll often find more spots than you otherwise might. Maybe the guy on your left will always defend his blinds, discouraging you from raising with junk when you're in the small blind or on the button, but a raise from the cutoff (the seat just to the right of the dealer) will almost always get him—and the two play-ers to his left—to fold without a fight. You might find that the woman on your right loves to raise with almost any two cards—but will check and fold if the flop misses her hand—and decide to smooth call every time she raises, then bet when she checks the flop.

The Middle is the part of the tournament when you can be your most creative—you're free from the tight constraints of the Beginning, and you're not as locked into decisions as you are during the Endgame. If you've been paying attention to the people at your table, you can really start to play the player instead of cards.

The "Crazy" Call

One of the main reasons I like to double up early in a tournament is that it allows me to take some chances during the middle and late stages. There are times, I'll admit, that these chances make me look like I've com-pletely lost my mind. But there is, of course, a method to my madness.

When faced with calling a raise, the first thing I'll do is look down at my stack and figure out the repercussions.

If I call and win, I'll have x amount of chips.

If I call and lose, I'll have y amount of chips.

If I fold, I'll have z amount of chips.

When calling and losing will leave me in relatively the same posi-tion as folding—that is, y is relatively close to z—I'll give serious thought to making the call. If the conditions are favorable and the upside (the "x factor") is substantial, then the actual cards I'm holding are almost irrelevant.

Here's a good example: Last year, I found myself among the final nine players in the Ultimate Poker Challenge, a $3,000 buy-in no-limit Hold'em event at the Plaza in Las Vegas. While all nine of us were seated at the same table, the tournament was structured so that only seven would make the televised final table.

With the blinds at $800/$1,600 with $200 antes, I had about $80,000 in chips, twice the size of the average stack at the table. Michael "The Grinder" Mizrachi opened with a small raise to $3,500; David Singer called. Sitting in the cutoff, I looked down to find J-10 and decided to call. T.J. Cloutier, seated to my left in the small blind, pushed all-in with his remaining chips, about $20,000. The big blind, down to his last $4,000 or so and pretty much pot-committed to call with whatever he had left, did exactly that.

The Grinder and Singer both folded, leaving me to make a decision. Should I call another $16,500 in chips? I went into my routine ...

If I call and win, I'll have over $110,000 in chips, or about one-third of the chips in play. I will have succeeded in knocking out two players (including one of the most formidable tournament players in the history of poker), making the televised table, and forging a substantial chip lead over my opponents. If I call and lose, I'll have about $60,000 in chips. I'll still be the chip leader with a well-above average stack, large enough (with about 40 big blinds) to stay in my comfort zone. And if I fold, I'll have just under $76,500 in chips. Still the chip leader, well above the average, and more than enough to stay in my comfort zone.

As you can see, a win here would carry a lot of upside, while the difference between a call-and-lose and a fold wouldn't affect my comfort level in any significant way. I decided to call the bet.

T.J. turned over A-K, while the big blind showed 10-9. My plan seemed to be working to perfection when the flop came jack high, but T.J. caught a king on the river to win the pot. Afterward, he grumbled at me. "Kind of a crazy call with jack-ten."

Maybe so. But those are the kinds of calls that let you build a $100,000 stack into a $600,000 stack late in a tournament without taking on too much risk. You are not going to negatively affect your ability to control your own destiny and—if things break right—you'll gain enough chips to exert even greater control over the table, build momentum, and enjoy a feeling (at least until the next hand) of invincibility. Greg "Fossilman" Raymer used this kind of thinking to perfection, making (and usually benefiting from) these kinds of decisions as he blazed his way to the 2004 World Series championship, a feat he came amazingly close to duplicating in 2005.

Keep in mind that I'm *not* advocating making these "crazy" calls during the early part of a tournament, when your chips are usually way too precious to take on this kind of risk, or in cash games, when there's little upside to knocking opponents out or becoming the chip leader. But in the later stages of a tournament, when massive swings of fortune accompany nearly every showdown, being a little crazy might be the only reasonable thing to do.

The Bubble

While poker tournaments are usually full of exciting and terrifying moments, the tension really thickens as players approach the bubble.

It's only natural. Although they can last for hours, even days, multi-table tournaments are basically all-or-nothing propositions. Either you make the money or you don't. And if you don't, it's easy to convince yourself that you've wasted your time and money.

The bubble is the make-or-break time. Make a mistake and you're going home empty-handed. So why not let other people make the mistakes? All you have to do is play conservatively for a while, staying out of trouble until the last remaining unlucky souls have busted themselves out of the tournament ...

The problem with this thinking, of course, is that poker favors the bold. When everybody else is tightening up, avoiding any confrontation without a premium hand, the good players do exactly the opposite, firing away, stealing every blind, ante, and pot they can get their hands on.

Why do they expose themselves to this kind of risk? It's simple: the prize structure. The guy who squeezed past the bubble to finish 560th in the 2005 WSOP Championship made $12,500, a 25 percent return on the $10,000 entry fee. The guy who finished first won $7,500,000, a 750 percent return on his investment. In other words, Mr. 560 would have to squeeze past the bubble in a multi-table tournament *every single day for more than eight years* before earning as much as the first-place finisher did in a single effort.

It's usually much, much more lucrative to win a tournament than to make the money, so much so that it's worth risking everything to improve your chances of winning it all.

Keep in mind, however, that this concept is hardly a secret. Some players will tighten up as the bubble approaches, while others will loosen their games. The trick is determining which approach each player has adopted, allowing you to pick your best spots. Against an aggressive player, you may be able to reraise with almost anything. When a conservative player raises, however, you may want to consider laying down that A-K!

> **Don't let the approach of the bubble send you into hiding. In the long run, you are going to be much better off using your opponents' passivity as an opportunity to try to increase your stack with aggressive play, putting yourself in a better position to make serious money once the bubble breaks.**

The Endgame

The closing stages of a tournament—especially the final table—should look very familiar to you: It's kind of like a Sit-N-Go.

There are some differences, of course. Since everyone will be starting with a different number of chips, you have to be aware of what each player will likely be trying to accomplish. Short stacks will obviously be looking to survive, trying to find places to push all-in and hoping to double up. Big stacks will either be playing ultraconservatively, waiting for a big hand, or applying relentless pressure, raising often in an attempt to steal the blinds and antes. Players with average stacks will probably be looking for low-risk, high-reward opportunities and may be more vulnerable to bluffs or other aggressive moves that force them to make decisions involving a lot of chips.

Which strategy will you use? All of them! When you have a sense of how someone is likely to be playing, it's usually to your advantage to do the opposite. Loosen up against the tight players, bluff the conservatives, and stay out of the way of loose, aggressive players with big stacks unless you've got the goods (or enough fold equity) to make a big reraise. Attack the average stacks! The key to succeeding in this part of the tournament is changing gears at the right times, anticipating what your opponent is going to do one step before he does.

Short-Stack Strategy

Changing gears may sound like a great strategy, but it assumes that you have enough chips to choose among different styles of play. You'll often find yourself at the other end of the spectrum, clinging to a short stack that allows you only to make one move: all-in.

There's no point to letting your chips get blinded off haphazardly, putting yourself in a position where you've got to win six hands in a row just to get back into contention—you might as well take advan-

> **Don't wait too long to start pushing all-in with a short stack—you're in a far better position when your raise still has some fold equity, and even if someone calls with a better hand, you'll always have a chance to draw out!**

tage of fold equity when you've got it. When you get down to eight big blinds or less, you want to start looking for spots to move all-in before the flop, hopefully taking the blinds and antes without a showdown.

Even if you get called, it's hard to be worse than a 3-to-1 underdog. If that sounds bad to you, look at it this way: It's about as easy to win one hand as a 3-to-1 underdog as it is to win three consecutive hands as a 2-to-1 favorite! In other words, you're usually just as well off risking eight big blinds as an underdog as you'd be trying to fight back from two big blinds with great cards.

Let's face it—no matter how good you are, you have to get lucky to win a tournament, especially in the later stages. The important thing is to play without any fear. If you can train your mind to win instead of just trying not to lose, the cards will often find ways to reward you.

> **If you can train your mind to win instead of just trying not to lose, the cards will often find ways to reward you.**

Heads-Up Play

How important is heads-up play? Let's put it this way: How are you going to win a tournament without it? Yes, there are very rare occasions when you'll knock out your last two opponents on a single hand—Phil

Gordon did it at the 2004 Bay 101 Shooting Stars tournament—but most of the time you're going to have to defeat a single player, mano a mano, in order to win.

Fortunately—thanks once again to online poker—it's easier than ever to practice heads-up play. Most sites offer both cash games and Sit-N-Gos that let you face off against a single opponent. Playing in these games is well worth the time, not just because they're a perfect way to get better, but because heads-up play is fun.

The old adage about "playing the player, not the cards" doesn't get any truer than it does in a head-to-head matchup. Heads-up play is poker at its purest, rewarding in equal parts your fearlessness, hand-reading skills, patience, instincts, and ability to tell a convincing story.

The strategy you decide to use in a heads-up match really depends on two basic Factors: the size of the stacks relative to the blinds and the strategy your opponent has chosen to use.

The first Factor is the easier one to identify. You'll often wind up in a situation where the blinds and antes represent such a significant part of your stack that you'll be pretty much committed to any pot you enter. In these situations, all you can do is find a hand that looks like it has a reasonable chance of being the best and move all your chips into the middle.

Heads-up play is much more interesting when you *don't* have to risk all your chips on a single hand, giving each player the chance to outplay the other. As I said earlier, the most important thing to do is identify the strategy that your opponent is using.

Heads-up strategy tends to move along a spectrum between two extremes. The aggressive approach is to frequently jam the pot with big raises, forcing your opponent to make a decision for all his chips on nearly every hand. The subtler approach—and the one I happen to prefer—is to keep the pots small and to chip away at your opponent's stack.

Why do I prefer the second approach? Because it's too easy to double up your opponent in heads-up play. Let's say I have $800,000 to my opponent's $200,000. A 4-to-1 chip advantage might seem like a lot, but if he goes all-in and wins against me, my advantage is reduced to 3-to-2. If he can do it again on the next hand, suddenly it's me facing the 4-to-1 chip disadvantage!

When I keep the pots small—limping instead of raising, keeping my bets and raises small—my opponent can't double up against me. By playing more pots, I can also protect myself against the whims of short-term luck: My opponent may pick up a huge hand or deliver a bad beat once or twice, but he's going to have a hard time doing it 20 or 30 times. It's a strategy that drives a lot of my opponents crazy. "You never call me when I have a big hand!"

Of course, this strategy only works against a player from whom I can take a lot of small pots. The best way to combat any heads-up strategy is usually to do exactly the opposite. If I am trying to keep the pots small, a smart opponent will raise me almost every time, forcing me to play bigger pots.

This is why it's so important to identify your opponent's strategy as quickly as possible. Pay close attention to the size of his bets in relation to the blinds and the size of the pot. Take note of whether he likes to call, then lead out with a bet on the flop, or if he's a habitual check-raiser. It's often worth it early in a match to call your opponent down

> **The best heads-up strategy is often to do the opposite of what your opponent is doing. It's sometimes a good idea, early in a heads-up match, to call your opponent down with a mediocre hand if it will give you a clearer picture of the way he has decided to play against you.**

to the river with next to nothing if you can learn a little more about the types of cards he's playing and the way he's playing them.

Keep in mind that your opponent is also trying to get a handle on the way *you* are playing. This means you can't ever get too committed to any single strategy—you're going to have to change gears when the situation demands it, hopefully staying one step ahead of your opponent.

But that's what makes heads-up play so much fun: The "science" of poker gets thrown out the window, giving your inner poker artist a chance to have his fun. I am always looking for opportunities to improve my heads-up skills, whether by practicing or by observing others.

Mark Seif

If you've ever played in a big Sunday online tournament, you've played against Mark Seif. And he probably fared a lot better than you did. Mark is an incredibly astute online poker player—on Absolute Poker he goes by "Mark Seif," and on PokerStars he's "Buster Love"—who, as he'll tell you, "never takes a hand off." In 2005, he managed to eclipse his superb online results with an incredible run at the World Series of Poker, winning two gold bracelets and placing in the money in a third event. I have no doubt that his mastery of online tournaments played a huge role in his success against the increasingly large fields at the WSOP.

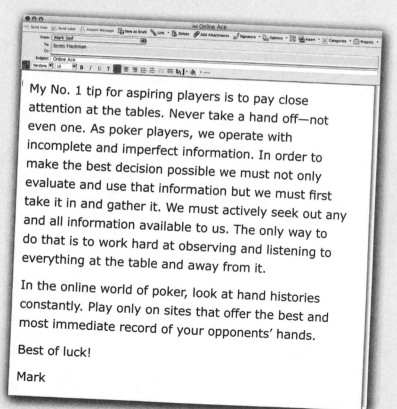

My No. 1 tip for aspiring players is to pay close attention at the tables. Never take a hand off—not even one. As poker players, we operate with incomplete and imperfect information. In order to make the best decision possible we must not only evaluate and use that information but we must first take it in and gather it. We must actively seek out any and all information available to us. The only way to do that is to work hard at observing and listening to everything at the table and away from it.

In the online world of poker, look at hand histories constantly. Play only on sites that offer the best and most immediate record of your opponents' hands.

Best of luck!

Mark

CHAPTER SEVEN:
Multi-Tabling

TOURNAMENT POKER MAY BE the most exciting way to play the game, but it's not necessarily the most profitable. For every World Series champion like Joseph Hachem, there are more than 5,000 players who didn't finish in the money and maybe millions of others who took a shot at a satellite or a supersatellite and failed to earn a ticket.

Regardless of how good a player you are, you have to get lucky to win a tournament. Even if you had the ability to read minds and risked all your chips only in situations where you were an 80 percent favorite to win, the odds say you'd still lose one out of every five confrontations.

Take a moment to ponder this: You could decide to play *only* pocket aces during a tournament and get lucky enough to find them a half-dozen times. Let's say you raise with them each time, only to get reraised all-in by someone with a hand much worse than yours. It would almost certainly be mathematically correct to call each of these reraises, and more likely than not, you'd go home a loser.

Professionals understand how hard it is to win a tournament. That's why they play so many of them. It seems like I am constantly on the move, traveling from city to city, to places as different as Indiana and Monaco.

Obviously, it's incredibly fun, but it's also extremely expensive. Aside from entry fees, there are the flights, the hotels, and the food. All combined with the chance—make that *likelihood*—that I won't make any money at all for my time and effort during any individual tournament.

Understanding Variance

Many new players—especially after logging a decent win or two—tend to underestimate just how crazy luck can be. No matter how good a player you are, you are going to encounter bad luck. Really bad luck. Utterly ridiculous shit luck. I shudder to think of the number of poor mice that I have smashed, thrown, or otherwise destroyed because my aces full were cracked for the seventh consecutive time by a runner-runner straight flush.

What you've got to remember is that streaks—lucky and unlucky— are a normal part of the game. They are part of a larger concept called variance, which means that the road to average is full of all kinds of wild twists and turns. In other words, even if you are playing well enough to be a consistent winner at your game or games of choice, you are still going to suffer through periods when nothing seems to be going your way.

There are, however, two bits of good news. First, variance works both ways—even a mediocre poker player will enjoy the occasional winning streak while good players will enjoy runs where every decision seems to result in a jackpot payday. The second is that losing streaks—at least the kinds associated with variance—are just temporary diseases whose cure really isn't that unpleasant: Just play more hands. Solid play will eventually correct whatever damage has been done to your bankroll.

And what if your losing streak isn't just an ordinary fluctuation of luck? I'll address some ideas for dealing with your more serious slides later in this chapter.

Embracing Variance

One of the many great things about online poker is that there's a simple way to attack variance—by embracing it.

Anyone who has spent significant time playing poker in brick-and-mortar casinos has experienced a night where nothing goes right. You don't get dealt a playable hand for three hours. You get pocket aces four times in an hour and lose each time. You can't make a draw to save your life. Your opponents are hitting draws that you didn't even realize were possible. Poker can be a brutal game.

You're going to experience the same bad beats online, but—thanks to the speed of the game—it will take less real time to pull out of a losing streak. And when you're comfortable, you can shorten the time even further by playing more than one table at the same time.

This strategy has its critics, of course. You're not going to be able to focus on a couple of critical Factors, namely table image (yours

---

Multi-tabling allows you to maximize the number of hands you see, minimizing the effects of variance and creating results that more accurately reflect your level of skill.

---

and everybody else's) and your opponents' out-of-the-box plays. As a result, you're likely to miss a few potentially profitable spots.

I strongly believe, though, that if you're playing solid poker—a style I like to call Robot poker—the advantages outweigh the drawbacks. Let's say you're consistently earning three bets an hour in your regular game, and you calculate that you owe one of those bets to the careful attention you direct toward your opponents. So what happens if you add a second table? Your earn rate may go down to two bets an hour per table, but overall you'll be taking in four bets an hour. Add a third table, and you'll be making six bets.

This strategy only works if you've actually mastered the game you're trying to play. Remember the blackjack example earlier? A player who makes only one or two mistakes an hour counting cards will actually lose *more* money than a non-card counter using basic blackjack strategy. The same thinking applies to multi-tabling: Any flaws in your game are going to be magnified with each table you add. Hard-earned bankrolls can be wiped out with frightening speed.

Your best results from multi-tabling come when you are able to play solid, consistent poker without any in-the-moment acknowledgment of the results. Residual anger over a bad beat at one table can easily infect your decision making at another table, making for a very expensive session.

If you're starting to get the sense that multi-tabling can be a little dangerous, good. I'm trying to keep you on your toes. Make sure that

> **Your best results from multi-tabling come when you are able to play solid, consistent poker without any in-the-moment acknowledgment of the results.**

each time you add a new table, you are doing so within your comfort zone. Don't add a second table until you've mastered the Factors associated with playing the first. Don't add a third table until you've mastered playing two, etc.

By the way, there's no rule stating that you've got to play all these games on the same site. If you find comfortable games across a number of different sites, the same concepts apply.

I don't, however, recommend playing different games. It's very hard to make consistently good, in-the-moment decisions when you are juggling two cash games, two full tournaments, and two Sit-N-Gos. The same applies to mixing Hold'em with stud with Omaha with badugi. Don't force yourself to process several different sets of Factors at the same time; stick to games that allow you to use the same basic criteria to choose the best course of action.

So proceed with caution, but don't underestimate the power of multi-tabling. In an instant-gratification world, it's the best way to see long-term results in the short term.

The Robot

Zen masters call it "being in the moment." Or maybe it's "not being." I don't know. I'm not a Zen master. I call it the Robot.

The Robot plays online poker like it's a videogame—almost mindlessly, with his brain shut off. He doesn't worry about his opponents, because there are no opponents, just patterns. The Robot can identify a pattern and respond appropriately without having to think about it. It doesn't matter to the Robot whether he's won the last five hands or lost the last 30, except to the extent that it affects the patterns—he is going to make the right play every time.

Yes, the Robot may be sacrificing a little bit of equity by not playing the player. After all, the Robot responds to tried-and-true patterns, not to the way Player X has been playing for the last five hours, and in doing so, he may miss a few opportunities to snap off bluffs or make a *value bet*. But online poker offers a golden opportunity that more than compensates for the loss: The Robot can play more than one table at a time. And the more hands the Robot sees, the more money he makes.

Above all, the Robot has no emotions. He doesn't live and die with every card. There is no bad beat that can put him on tilt or cold run of cards that will change the way he plays. There is only the satisfaction that comes with being a properly functioning Robot, always making the right play in the right situation.

It might sound like the Robot has a pretty boring life. Maybe so. But the Robot only has to act robotic at the table. He's free to do whatever he wants at the end of his poker session with all of the money he's won.

Be the Robot.

Running Bad

You have to lose. You have to have downswings. It's a normal part of the game.

Running bad is a condition that begins when a player in the midst of an otherwise normal downswing starts to make adjustments to his style that wind up exacerbating a losing streak.

Sometimes these adjustments are conscious—"I never win with ace-king, so I'm going to stop raising with it before the flop." The more insidious adjustments are the ones you don't realize you're making, usually involving playing more hands ("That guy's winning with 5-4 offsuit; maybe I can too!") with less aggression ("He's been bad-beating me all day, so I'm just going to check instead of betting").

How do you know when a slip is becoming a slide? It's not easy, especially if you're struggling to maintain a positive attitude in the face of a downswing. "I'm just getting unlucky" is a statement that, even if it's true, can be used to mask all kinds of errors on the part of the person making it.

This is one of the reasons it's so critical for new players to keep detailed records of their play. By examining your past results, you can usually distinguish between a normal downswing and a self-induced case of poor play.

What can you do if you suspect that you're running badly? Here are a few suggestions:

TIGHTEN UP AND GET MEAN!
Many severe losing streaks are created by one (or worse, a combination) of two conditions: playing too many hands and playing too passively. There's nothing wrong with playing tight, "raise-or-release" poker until you're feeling comfortably back on track.

EXAMINE THE GAME CONDITIONS
Good poker players love the bad ones. After all, they're the ones fueling the poker economy! Unfortunately poker is a zero-sum game, and eventually the sheep get too tired (or too broke) to get sheared. Losing one or two "producers" from your regular game can put a severe dent in your earning power. What's worse, you may discover that the presence of these bad players has been masking a few leaks in your own game that now need fixing. (We'll come back to leaks in a minute.)

An influx of bad players can cause even more problems than their departure. Your raises won't be as effective, and you might as well forget about bluffing. Take some time to see if and how the game conditions may have changed, and experiment with changing your strategy accordingly.

EXAMINE YOURSELF
Running badly tends to create negative emotions, which in turn tend to aggravate the bad run. Take a long, honest look at yourself to make sure that you're playing your A-game.

149

Daniel Negreanu once wrote a great article for *Card Player* magazine about how his game became severely affected by what began with a glass of wine with his meal and turned into a liquid dinner. Maybe you're playing when you're tired or stressed. Maybe you've started turning on the TV in the background or IMing your friends while you play. Or you're stressing about work, your finances, your relationship, your dog.

Your strongest opponent at the table is often your own behavior. Make sure you're always giving yourself the best opportunity to focus and play your best game.

SWITCH GAMES

One of my favorite cures for running bad is to switch to a different game. A bad run at Hold'em? I'd play stud. Stud no good? Move on to Omaha, then back to Hold'em, etc. (Ideally, at this point you're proficient in a handful of games and can change with relative ease.)

Switching games forces me to rethink my strategy, as I have to remember (or learn) what it takes to win. By the time I've returned to the game I was running badly at, I've hopefully "unlearned" whatever bad habits were causing me to lose.

SWITCH SITES ... OR TAKE A VACATION!

The problem with any routine is that it's easy for bad habits to become part of the ritual. Sometimes a change of scenery—something as small as a different "ping" when I make a bet—is enough to shake me out of the doldrums.

And in the case of a really bad run, it's often a good idea to take a vacation from the game altogether. As I said earlier, running bad can lead to negative thinking, which usually leads to more running bad. A week or two away from poker can often give you the time and space you need (as we learned from *Happy Gilmore*) to find your happy place.

Leaks

Everyone makes mistakes. Excruciatingly stupid, "I can't believe I just did that, I have got to be the biggest idiot in the world" mistakes. I will sometime agonize for days after making a dumb decision that gets me knocked out of a major tournament.

When you are multi-tabling, however, you don't have time to wallow in your mistakes. Another hand is usually starting before you are able to process the one you just finished. This can be a good thing, as you won't have the opportunity to dwell too long in a negative place—there's always a new pot on the horizon! But without self-reflection, it's much easier to make the same mistake two or three times. Or a dozen.

Poker players call them leaks, little mistakes that may cost you a bet or two and are easily forgotten. The problem is that when you are multi-tabling, little mistakes add up in a hurry, costing you hundreds, maybe thousands of dollars.

Regardless of whether you are winning or losing, it's important to always be examining your game for leaks. Here are a few of the most common ones:

CALLING RAISES

You can take a lot more chances in a ring game—when a replenished bankroll is only a click away—than in a tournament, where your primary concern is survival. Calling raises against players who you think you can outplay after the flop can be not only profitable but sexy! But what may be a great play in the moment can quickly become a bad habit—you've got to give players credit for having hands at least some

---

It's almost always better to be the one raising than the one calling the raise.

---

of the time, and there's a fine line between being an opportunist and a calling station.

UNDERESTIMATING OPPONENTS

As I said earlier, most poker players think they're better than average, and they can't all be right. It's easy, especially after a couple of bad beats, to start thinking of all your opponents as donkeys. They aren't. Almost everyone has an A-game, even if they choose not to use it all of the time.

I'm most successful at multi-tabling when I play as if all my opponents are solid players against whom I have to make good decisions.

OVERESTIMATING OPPONENTS

While all your opponents won't be donkeys, most of them won't be top pros, either. A lot of the sophisticated trickery you see on TV—setting traps, making daring bluffs—won't work against the opponents you encounter online. They may not understand that they're being bluffed. They may, like you, be multi-tabling and paying almost zero attention to your table image. Your most consistent profits online will come from playing straightforward, aggressive poker. Save the trickery for the televised table.

OVERVALUING ACES

When the cards aren't flowing your way, hands like A-J or A-10 can start to seem like powerhouses. They aren't. They're usually underdogs to the kinds of hands your opponents will raise with, especially if those hands are bigger aces. And they're almost impossible to get away from when an ace appears on the flop. Frequently playing "weak" aces is a good way to rack up significant losses.

By the way, this advice also extends to pocket aces. While you'd never think about throwing them away before the flop in a cash game, there are plenty of flops that will transform your "rockets" into two

worthless scraps of paper. There's no shame in slowing down or folding when it seems likely that you're beaten. Remember what they say:
Pocket aces are good for winning small pots...and losing big ones!

OVERVALUING SUITED CARDS

When you're looking at six new hands a minute, finding two suited cards
can be a little like comfort food: the first thing you reach for when you
don't want to think.

While being suited helps, it should never be the primary reason
for playing a hand. You're only going to flop a flush about one time in
120. It's a lot easier to flop four cards to a flush (about 1 in 9), putting
yourself in a position to spend your money in the hopes that the fifth
flush card will show up by the river, something that's going to happen
less than half the time you are in that situation. When you do make
your flush, it's usually so obvious that your action will dry up immediately ... unless someone has a bigger flush!

**Treat suited cards as a bonus. But don't
let the color of the cards get in the way of
playing them intelligently.**

IGNORING POSITION

Position is one of the most important Factors in poker. It's also one of
the most overlooked. While you may have discovered a few tricks for
getting around a positional disadvantage—a well-timed check-raise,
or an all-in bet—remember that it is still a disadvantage. You are
going to win a lot more money and, more important, lose a lot less
when you are the player with superior position.

The most common form of position abuse comes from the blinds. It's easy to call a half-bet from the small blind or a raise from the big, even though you are going to be in the worst possible position throughout the remainder of the hand. The truth is that most players, regardless of their skill level, are lifetime losers when playing from the blind.

RESTRAINING AGGRESSION

You will encounter many situations where you have to decide between a passive course of action (checking or calling) and a more aggressive tactic (betting or raising). It's natural to take the easy way out when you're in the midst of five different games: "I can't lose too much money by calling."

That may be true for any particular situation, but those situations add up in a hurry. Consistently costing yourself the equity you might gain from raising instead of calling will eventually take a big chunk out of your bankroll. If you're playing too many tables to play aggressive poker, then you are playing too many tables.

WINNING

Huh? How can winning be a leak? Well, maybe it's less a leak than a "leak enabler." You can enjoy winning sessions, even winning months during periods when you're guilty of playing suboptimal poker. Don't let winning mask physical or psychological fatigue, laziness, or some other decline in your decision-making abilities. Hey, even Robots need tune-ups every once in a while. Make your adjustments *before* you start losing. It's a lot easier to lose your winnings than it is to recoup your losses.

Stepping Back

If we were really Robots with unlimited processing capacity, we could keep adding table after table to the mix, increasing our positive expectations without any limit. We are not Robots, of course, and everybody has a limit. Your game may fall apart after you add a third table. Or a 10th. If you're anything like me, you are going to keep pushing those limits until they start to push back at you, forcing you to return to whatever level you were previously able to manage.

There's no shame in scaling back. If you were a consistent winner playing three tables at once but lost a bundle after adding a fourth, then go back to three.

This may seem like a no-brainer, so much so that many people forget to tell their brains, which are still operating as if there were more tables in play. Moving from four tables to three can make you feel like a junkie trying to quit—once you've become accustomed to the action, there's a transition involved in scaling back.

I experience this all the time when I move from, say, multi-tabling five games to a single, big buy-in tournament. I quickly discover that I'm paying *too* much attention. I start to notice tiny things that I never would have noticed before—"false" Factors—that lead me to make bad decisions.

Junkies have methadone; you have TV. An iPod. The phone. This is the only time when I think it's okay to allow extra distractions into your environment, and even then only until your brain activity slows down to a point when you can direct an appropriate amount of focus— not too much, not too little—on the game in front of you.

Thomas "Thunder" Keller

The first time I saw Thomas Keller, he was sitting in Seat 1 at the 2004 WPT Celebrity Invitational. With his bleached blond curls and bubbly sense of humor (and the fact that we were in LA), I was sure he was an actor.

The next time I saw him, he was being handed a gold bracelet for winning the $5,000 no-limit Hold'em event at the 2004 World Series of Poker. I remember thinking to myself, Pretty good for an actor!

I later discovered that "Thunder" was actually a fearsome Internet poker star. I hadn't seen him at many tournaments because he was too busy crushing online cash games. Thomas and I went on to become great friends—he taught me as much about being a person as a poker player, and even backed me for a while. If you want to play online cash games, look no further than Thomas.

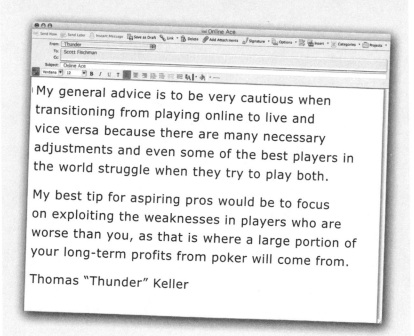

My general advice is to be very cautious when transitioning from playing online to live and vice versa because there are many necessary adjustments and even some of the best players in the world struggle when they try to play both.

My best tip for aspiring pros would be to focus on exploiting the weaknesses in players who are worse than you, as that is where a large portion of your long-term profits from poker will come from.

Thomas "Thunder" Keller

CHAPTER EIGHT:
Beyond Texas Hold'em

POCKET ACES. THE FLOP. The turn. The river. Seems like you can't go anywhere these days without hearing someone talk about Texas Hold'em.

Talk to anyone who played poker before, say, 1990, and you might be surprised to hear that once upon a time people played games other than Hold'em. In fact, one of the reasons it initially became so popular among professionals is that there were so few people who knew how to play it well.

That certainly isn't the case anymore. Inspired by the huge paydays and massive TV coverage, it seems like everyone knows what to do with pocket queens before the flop. An unofficial survey of the airwaves and the shelves at my local bookstore reveals that something like 95 percent of all the televised tournaments and books out there focus on Hold'em.

But there are a lot of smart reasons to learn other games.

IT'S A GOOD CURE FOR RUNNING BAD

Dropping down from a $15/$30 to a $3/$6 Hold'em game in the midst of an extended losing streak might make you feel like a loser. But taking up $3/$6 stud, well, that's an *experiment*.

OTHER GAMES ARE FUN

Like to play "action" Hold'em, seeing flops with a lot of different hands? Then you'll probably *love* Omaha, especially the hi-lo variety. Sick of having to throw away every hand immediately after seeing the flop? Try seven-card stud, where it's often good business to pay to see an extra card or two to see what develops.

IT'S A BADGE OF HONOR

When the greatest poker players in the world gather for the "big game" at the Bellagio, they're often playing a $2,000/$4,000 "mixed" game, switching forms of poker from round to round. For an old-school pro, it's a point of pride to excel at *all* forms of poker, not just the game that's most popular today.

IT'S A LOT EASIER TO WIN A TOURNAMENT!

Well, that may not be entirely true, but the tournament fields are usually smaller. When Greg "Fossilman" Raymer won the $10,000 no-limit Hold'em event at the 2004 World Series, he had to outwit, outdraw, and outlast 2,575 other players. I had to face less than one-tenth that many on my way to winning a gold bracelet in the $2,000 H.O.R.S.E (Hold'em, Omaha, Razz, Seven-Card Stud Hi and Hi-Lo Eight-or-Better) event.

As I've said, though, I think it's a bad idea—no, make that a train wreck of an idea—to start playing all forms of poker at the same time. Just as you would with multi-tabling, try one game at a time until you feel like you've recognized all (or at least enough) of the Factors associated with it.

And when embarking on a new game, give serious thought to the idea of starting with tournaments. You'll not only gain exposure to shifting strategies but you'll have a built-in stop-loss on the "cost" of your education. The price you'll pay to see an hour's worth of hands in a $10 buy-in stud tournament is probably a huge bargain compared with what you'll spend in the same length of time at a cash table.

The descriptions that follow are in no way meant to be comprehensive strategy guides to any of the games I've included; they're merely a few of the Factors you might want to consider when branching out into a new game. I've also included the rules of each game in the appendices.

Seven-Card Stud

Seven-card stud used to be the most popular poker game around. Sadly, this is no longer the case, but it's still a very intriguing game, providing an observant player with more information than virtually any other form of poker.

The reason for this is pretty obvious: You get to see more cards. In Hold'em, when all the cards are out, you know seven of them. In an eight-handed stud game, you'll know 10 cards before you have to make your first decision.

The structure of the game also demands that players—at least the good ones—stick to a narrower range of starting hands. In Hold'em, a single bet before the flop will let you see five of the seven cards you are going to have to make your hand. The structure of most limit Hold'em games will let you see a sixth card if you're willing to pay a small bet. Stud, on the other hand, places two rounds of betting between you and the fifth card, and a sixth card is likely to cost you a double bet. As a result, you've got to be much more selective about the hands you choose to invest in—the "Any two will do!" spirit that can dominate many Hold'em games is largely absent at the stud table.

A player who has voluntarily entered a pot almost always has one of two kinds of hands: a pair (or trips) or grouped cards that can used to make flushes and/or straights. The first and maybe most revealing Factor in stud poker comes when you can determine how an opponent likes to open with each of them.

Many stud players like to raise with their pairs or trips and limp in with their draws. This is an incredibly powerful piece of information. For example, an opponent who limped in with a 7 proceeds to catch a 6 and a 9. He bets into me.

In Hold'em, if a player showed aggression with a 6-7-9 board, I'd have to consider the possibility I was facing a straight. Against most stud opponents, however, I can be pretty sure that the opposite is true—would he really have played J-10-8? Since he limped into this pot, he probably didn't start with a split pair of 7s or hidden pair of 9s. His behavior suggests that he started with something like 7-8-9, choosing to bet after pairing his 9 on fifth street. As long as I can represent something better than a pair of 9s, I can raise him.

Or the same player limps in with a 10, then pairs it on fourth street. Does he have three 10s? Probably not. But you would be amazed at the lengths some some players will take to bluff me into thinking they've got trips in this situation. Since my opponent's paired board allows me to make a double bet on fourth street (this is a very important rule that a lot of new players forget to take advantage of), his attempted bluff may wind up earning me a few extra bets.

Obviously, not every player is so straightforward, but there are plenty of other pieces of information available to you. As I mentioned earlier, you begin knowing 10 cards—your two holes cards and the eight door cards. You'll use this knowledge, of course, to figure out how many of the cards that will help you are live, aiding you in gauging the strength of your hand. More importantly, your opponents will be doing the same thing! If the door cards include two 7s and a 3, and someone enters the action with a 6 showing, you can pretty much guarantee that he's not on a straight draw.

Your bluffs in a stud game have to be precise, fitting into a clearly defined set of parameters. It's hard to bluff a flush, for example, when your opponents know that most of the cards in your suit are dead. You've got to be a skilled storyteller to succeed at stud, because your target audience is going to be a lot more literate. It's going to be much easier to spot a hole in your plot.

Because there is so much information available in stud games, your bluffs have to be more precise.

While all of this available information can make it harder to bluff at stud, there are times when it makes it easier. Let's say I have an ace showing. Four players fold to me, I bet, and the player next to me raises me with a smaller door card. Does he have trips, or a killer draw? Maybe. Another possibility is that he has a hidden ace and knows that he has my hand "crippled." If so, he knows two things—I'm less likely to have a pair of aces, and even if I do, it's going to be harder for me to improve, making this a great spot for him to bluff me!

Reraising with the smaller door card is actually one of the most common bluffs you'll encounter at the stud table. It's rooted in fact—my opponent knows he has my hand crippled—and it's a huge show of strength: He's representing a hand bigger than the already big hand (aces) that I'm representing.

This kind of bluff, however, can easily backfire. Sure, he's got one of my aces, but I have his hand just as crippled. He can't be that strong either! And I can reraise with just about anything.

A lot of stud players get excited to find a big hidden pair in the hole. I get excited for them ... and for me, as this can be one of the most transparent hands to play against. For example, a tight player raises with a 7 on the door. There's already another 7 out, and maybe a couple of jacks and queens. I can now be pretty sure he's got hidden aces or kings. I am going to know how powerful he is on every street until the river. I can call him with a hand like 8-4-8 in the hopes of making a sneaky two pair and putting the hammer down on a later street.

The same reasoning demonstrates why it's difficult to play against a split pair of aces—you'll never know if and when your opponent pairs that second hole card. You could be "drawing dead" (or nearly so) from fourth street on.

Another critical Factor unique to stud poker is the moving button. Since the player with the strongest hand showing has to act first on each round, your betting position can change from street to street, making it harder to slowplay. A lot of the positional plays that you could make with the fixed button in Hold'em won't be available to you in stud. You can't check and call with the intention of check-raising on a later street, or raise in late position in the hopes of earning a free card, because by the time you get there, you may no longer be in the right position to pull it off.

An exception arises when a player pairs his door card on fourth street, showing a hand that is still likely to be best on fifth street. If that player leads out with a bet, you can take advantage of the "stuck" button to raise with a drawing hand in the hopes of getting a free look at sixth street. Even if your opponents suspect you are semi-bluffing, you are representing such a strong hand (and you don't seem to be afraid of the pair on the board) that it's hard for them to play back at you. And if they do, the extra bets in the pot will often improve your odds enough to make it correct to chase your draw all the way to the end of the hand.

I usually do pretty well in stud tournaments because the blind and ante structure not only rewards aggressive play, it also makes it mandatory, especially in the middle and late rounds. I'll play the early stages just like I would a Sit-N-Go—supertight, playing only premium hands. But once the antes kick up, I'll often (assuming I have enough chips) turn into a wild man, playing almost every hand at least all the way to fifth street.

As usual, my seeming insanity is rooted in rational thought. Let's say I'm playing in a limit stud tourney and have survived to see the middle rounds. The limits are $2,000/$4,000, with a $500 ante and a mandatory $1,000 bring-in for the low card. In other words, at an eight-player table, there will be $5,000 in the middle before I'm faced with a decision. My decision is pretty clear-cut: Raise to $2,000! Regardless of what I get called with, I am getting better than 3-to-1 odds on my money, good enough to continue with a wide range of hands.

I'll follow up with a bet on fourth street. Even if I'm heads-up, there will be at least $8,000 in the pot, giving me 4-to-1 odds even if I get called.

By fifth street, a relatively clear story has usually developed. Either my opponent buys what I'm selling and concedes the pot or he's determined to stick with his hand, in which case I can make a graceful exit (if I'm on a bluff) or keep him on the hook to win an even bigger pot (if I've got the goods). Sure, I'll lose a few of these hands, but as long as I take down a pot once every three or four times I play this way, I should come out ahead.

In other words, I'm getting great odds to attack every pot until fifth street with just about any hand. It's a relatively easy way to continue to build a stack in the later stages of a tournament without ever having to see a showdown. And when things are going my way, my junk hands will magically evolve into winners, giving me the chance to win some huge pots. I tend to hear some grumbling from opponents who accuse me of getting lucky, to which I say, "Of course I am!" But as long as I'm investing my money properly—taking advantage of the tremendous pot odds—it's more accurate to say that I am creating my own luck.

Seven-Card Stud Hi-Lo

This is probably my favorite form of poker because most players have trouble adjusting their strategies in the middle and late rounds. I only wish there were more than, say, three hi-lo tournaments a year.

My strategy for winning is in some ways the opposite of what I'll do in any other kind of tournament. In the early stages of a hi-lo tournament, there's not much point in aggressively playing a big pair, considered a premium hand in a regular stud tournament. You're not likely to get a lot of players to fold, and you'll be amazed at how many times an opponent sticking around in the hopes of winning the low end with a hand like 6-4-2 manages to back his way into a winning high hand such as two pair (or better). Even if my big pair does hold up, I'll often have to split the pot with the low hand. High risk, low reward. I'd much rather be the guy playing the 6-4-2.

Because there will be so many split pots during the early stages, it's very important to "jam" the pot early in a hand, making sure there's enough money in the middle to make a split worthwhile. Sometimes the best way to do that is to skip a raise that might otherwise thin the field. For example, say you've got a split pair of aces and you lead out with a bet. Three players call before the fourth, who has a 2 showing and raises. In almost any other form of poker, you would reraise here, thinning the field—they have to call a double bet—and possibly getting heads-up against the raiser. This raiser, however, looks like he's on a low draw, and there's not much value in being heads-up against him if you're going to wind up splitting your own money at the end. You want to keep those three players trapped between you. Call the bet, let everyone else call, then lead out with another bet on fourth street.

Keep in mind, though, that it's also easy to become the victim of someone else's jamming. Getting caught with a medium-strength hand you think might develop into a big hand can be very expensive if you find yourself stuck between players with high and low hands who keep raising each other. Save your chips for a better spot later.

Those better spots tend to spring up during the middle rounds of a tournament, when many players fail to acknowledge a tremendously significant change: There are fewer split pots. Because the bets have become so big, there are fewer callers and fewer actual showdowns. As long as you're not afraid to play your cards aggressively, you won't have to face too many low hands. I will definitely raise with my big pairs, and will play low hands only as the aggressor—pretty easy for me, as I'm raising almost every hand anyway!

It's amazing how many players fail to adjust to this simple change in strategy—and just how much you can profit from their mistake.

There will be a lot of split hands during the early stages of a hi-lo tournament, making it imperative to "jam" the pot with your good hands. Once you reach the middle stages, however, the number of split pots tends to tail off dramatically, a factor you should account for in your overall strategy.

Omaha Hi-Lo

Any guesses as to what poker game people will be playing when the Texas Hold'em craze dies down? I'd bet on Omaha.

If you love action, then Omaha hi-lo is the game for you. It seems like you can find a reason to play almost any hand you're dealt, and that every new card brings a dramatic shift in the balance of power.

My biggest hurdle when I first started playing this variation is that I played too tight. I'd rarely play a hand that didn't have an ace in it, and would never think of calling a raise with just an ace and a 4. When I began analyzing my results, one thing became clear: I sucked at this game.

Because Omaha is an action game with high rewards, you've got to be willing to take a little extra risk. In many cases, that means loosening up. Sure, double-suited aces (hands like A♥K♥A♠Q♠) are great, but so are hands like 2-3-5-6, as you've got a chance to "scoop" both the high and the low.

The most important factor in Omaha is probably board texture. Because you've got seven cards to work with after the flop, it's almost impossible not to have some kind of draw. The hard part is figuring out whether you actually want to make your hand.

For example, say you've got A♠ 3♠ 8♥ 9♥ and the flop comes:

K♠ 10♣ 7♦

At first glance, this looks like a pretty good flop for you: the 8 and 9 in your hand give you an open-ended straight draw. In Hold'em, you might play this aggressively, with reasonable confidence that a that a J or 6 will win you the pot. But do you really want to catch a jack in this situation? In Omaha hi-lo, players can almost always find a reason to play an ace. With four hole cards instead of two, it's almost three times as likely that someone has a queen to go with that ace, making a nut straight for them should the jack arrive. Nor is Q-9 out of the question. Even if no one has a better straight draw than you, the jack would create so many straight possibilities that you'd be unlikely to get any serious action. In other words, a great opportunity to win a small pot … or lose a big one!

It's not enough to keep track of your own outs, though—you have to pay close attention to the cards your opponents might be drawing to and determine how each out might affect a number of different hands.

With so much potential to make second- and third-best hands, a lot of players start to see dangers at every turn. I once found myself in a situation where an opponent was afraid to bet into me with a straight flush—because he was afraid that I had a bigger straight flush!

If I sit down at the table thinking, "I hope I make nut hands today," I know I'm in trouble. The game becomes a card-catching contest. Some days it will be—an opponent will make five nut hands against me and I will lose a bundle. I'll take my licks knowing that these days are the exceptions, though, not the rule.

It's actually a lot easier to play against tight Omaha players—the rocks who look for hands that give them two-way scoop opportunities and nut draws—because if they withstand any heat on the flop, I can usually guess at two or three of their hole cards. By playing looser than they do, I can create a wild table image that allows me to represent whatever I know they *don't* have. Let them draw at their nut hands—I'm more than happy to pick up all of the small pots.

In Omaha, I love to see flops like 10-10-4 or 9-9-9. Not only can I be pretty sure they've missed my tight opponents but my opponents— thanks to my "crazy" image—have to at least entertain the idea that those flops may have hit me. Even if they decide to "play sheriff" and call a bet or two, I can follow up with bets on later streets (as long as the board doesn't get too scary) to keep the pressure on—remember, a lot of these guys will lay down second- or third-nut hands.

This strategy works only against tight opponents, of course. Against the loose ones, I have to tighten up.

When you are playing Omaha hi-lo tournaments, keep in mind that, like in stud hi-lo, a low hand becomes less valuable in the middle to later stages of a tournament, as there will be fewer showdowns. Pre-flop aggression becomes extremely important, not just to eliminate showdowns but to thin the field as well. There are worse things than getting heads-up against a good player, even if you're holding junk—the possibility of a hi-lo split gives you a little extra equity in a shorthanded situation.

Razz

Talk to someone about Razz, and you're likely to hear one of two things:

"Never heard of it!"

"I hate that game!"

It's true, Razz—a variation of seven-card stud in which the low hand wins—can be one of the most frustrating games to play. It's also become incredibly hard to find, for a very simple reason: The bad players almost always lose. Razz, more than any other game, has fallen victim to the "bad player" paradox I mentioned in Chapter Five.

So why learn to play it? For one thing, you'll have to if you're going to succeed at H.O.R.S.E. or other mixed events.

Razz is a very cerebral game. You spend most of your time looking at your opponent's up cards and determining the best low hand they could have (an A-5 straight is the best possible hand). The ability to narrow the range of hands, however, makes it a very creative game: You can tell (or be told) a much more convincing story.

Because the range of winning hands is confined to just lows, it's usually pretty easy to put an opponent on a hand in Razz. A pre-flop raise with a 6 showing usually means an ace or a two in the hole. If that same opponent goes on to get dealt 2-A-K, you can usually be pretty sure that he's got a pair (bad, in Razz) and that your hand—or at least the hand you are representing—is a marginal favorite to win. In a cash game, this is usually a great time to get your money into the middle.

These marginally profitable situations make for tougher decisions in tournaments. You're ahead, but not by much, and with a limited supply of chips, you'd prefer situations that offer more in the way of value.

Razz is really a game for the poker connoisseur—which is, if you're in the right mind-set, what makes it interesting. When you've got two or three great players using Level 3 thinking to read and represent their hands, few games allow for more creativity.

Badugi!

While I'm generally not a huge fan of triple-draw games, I make an exception for badugi.

The goal of badugi is to draw to the best possible low hand with four cards. The twist is that you can use only one card from each suit, and you can't use pairs, forcing you to eliminate certain cards from your hand at showdown. A four-card hand—a "badugi"—is best, beating a three-card hand, which beats a two-card hand, etc. Trust me when I say that it isn't as confusing as it sounds, but you may want to read the complete set of rules I've included in the appendices.

Although badugi is technically a lowball game, you don't have to be afraid of high cards—it's much more important to avoid suited cards. For example, say I'm dealt

6♣ 7♦ 3♥ J♠

Badugi! But do I stand pat or discard the jack, hoping to draw a better spade?

The better question to ask is, "How likely are my opponents to outdraw me?" Let's say someone else is holding three different suits and discards one card, hoping to make a badugi. There are 13 cards in the deck that are of the suit he's looking for. But I am holding one of them. Two of them—the king and the queen—will make him a badugi worse than mine. Pairing any of the cards he's already holding will kill his badugi, thereby eliminating another three possibilities. In other words, he's down to seven outs, and we haven't even considered the possibility that there are other players in the hand—each of whom could be holding on to a card in his suit. Even though he has three draws to get to his card, the odds are stacked against him. My jack-high badugi will, more times than not, be good enough to win.

Now say I'm dealt

2♣ 9♠ K♦ Q♠

In most lowball games, if I decided to play a hand like this at all, I'd throw out the king and the queen. But as I pointed out above, it's more important in badugi to be unsuited than to rid myself of high cards. In this situation, I'll discard the queen but hold on to the king. If I wind up drawing another diamond, I can always throw the king away on the second or third draw.

Because it's so difficult to draw a clean out, my hand selection in badugi tends to be tighter than it would be in any other draw game. I will almost never play a hand that requires me to draw more than one card.

Finally, while this may be advice that applies to every kind of poker, it's incredibly important to pay attention to whatever information is available to you at the badugi table. I once found myself in a $100/$200 game where an opponent, frustrated by his inability to find a decent hand to play, showed off his cards as he discarded them: four spades. I looked down to find a hand that wasn't much better: three spades. As I was about to discard my seemingly useless cards, a lightbulb went off in my head: If we had seven spades between us, there were only six left in play. The odds of anyone having or drawing to a badugi were much smaller than normal. I realized I had a great bluffing opportunity and raised at the first opportunity, eventually taking the pot.

Sheets

If I had to thank one person for my success, it would be Eric Haber, a.k.a. Sheets. He not only hooked me up with the first backer willing to invest in me as a player but encouraged me—

What separates the good players from the great ones is their realization of the following truth: There is no truth. This is not meant to be a philosophy lecture, but a reminder that in every decision, there are a multitude of factors that must be considered before making the optimal play. What may be correct in one set of circumstances may be a complete blunder in an almost identical scenario with only one added variable.

There are probably about 300 things that could be considered before acting when it is your turn. I believe that the great players can identify and consider more of these factors in the time allotted than a good player can. It is only because so many of these factors have been worked out well in advance that it seems that they are acting so effortlessly and quickly when they are faced with a decision. So take your time with every decision and really consider all of the factors that could influence you. If you feel that there is more there than you can figure out in the time allotted, then do your best, write down the hand, and think about it more later. As in any profession, preparation is enormous.

ALWAYS be a student.

Sheets

both emotionally and financially—to branch out into games other than Texas Hold'em.

Aside from being a star in my sky, Eric has become a star in his own right, finishing in the money in several major events at the World Series and the World Poker Tour. He's also earned a well-deserved reputation as one of the most successful online tournament players in the known universe.

CHAPTER NINE:
Advanced Concepts

THERE ARE HUNDREDS OF millions of recreational poker players in the world. Only an infinitesimal number of them have what it takes to make a living as a professional poker player.

There are hundreds of reasons for not making it. Burnout. Depression. Boredom. Bad luck. Bad bankroll management. Bad life management.

As a professional, I get the chance to travel to a lot of interesting places, where I'll usually take a cab to a hotel, then to wherever the action is, then back to the airport. My "sightseeing," if I'm lucky, is generally limited to a few rounds at whatever golf course happens to be nearby.

Yes, the money is nice. Yes, I've made lots of incredible friendships. I also spend a good portion of the year living in hotel rooms. Most of my time is spent in cardrooms or in front of a computer. I don't have a serious girlfriend.

I'm not complaining. I wouldn't trade my life for any other. But *you* might. So before you quit your day job to become a professional poker player, consider the sacrifices you are going to have to make.

The great thing about online poker is that you can schedule the game around your life, not your life around the game.

Friends and Backers

I wouldn't be where I am without the help of my friends. There were those crazy Canadians I met in Reno who introduced me to the idea of playing online poker for a living. There was the Crew, who helped me elevate my game to an entirely new level. There is the network of players around the world I have met while playing the game who have become my closest friends.

Poker, at its heart, is a Darwinian game. The strong survive. Evolve or die. If you're not looking to improve your game—playing, thinking, analyzing, discussing—then the game is going to pass you by.

This creates a kind of paradox. While you've got to go it alone, competing against the world, you're spending all your time with the people you are competing against. They become your friends.

It's hard to remember at times, but poker is a game. The people you are stealing pots from today may be the people you're discussing hands with the next day.

♦ ♦ ♦

Winning two gold bracelets in 2004 was an amazing feeling. Not too far behind it: justifying the faith that my backers had in me. Without backers, I wouldn't have played in either event.

Sure, I had to split my winnings with them. In hindsight, however, I would have accepted backers—at least for the big-entry tournaments—who took *all* my winnings. The value of the experience itself—being able to compete against the best players in the world at some of the highest stakes available—was worth it.

I'm often asked how to find people to back you. I wish I had an answer better than "get lucky," but that's exactly what I did. I met Sheets through Brett "Gank" Jungblut. Sheets had backed Gank through a series of tournaments and seemed to like what he saw of the Crew. He hooked Dutch Boyd and me up with his business associate, Mark, who agreed to back us through a few events at the 2004 World Series.

Mark saw us as Hold'em specialists, and agreed to back us only in the Hold'em tournaments. Sheets agreed to pick up the slack, putting up the money for us to play in the non-Hold'em events.

The rest, as they say, is history: Gank cashed in five events, including a bracelet in Omaha hi-lo split. Dutch made the money in four, including a second-place finish in Razz. I cashed four times, winning twice, creating a little poetic justice along the way: The earnings from my Hold'em win were divvied up with Mark; the H.O.R.S.E. winnings were split with Sheets.

As I say, I was incredibly lucky to have found those guys, but I like to believe that I contributed to the creation of that luck. If I hadn't been preparing myself—living, eating, thinking, breathing poker—I never would have been able to take advantage of the opportunities that were presented to me.

Stop Keeping Records

I am a supercompetitive person. And there's nobody I compete with more fiercely than myself.

There is such a thing, however, as being too methodical. For me, there came a day several years ago when I discovered I was paying too much attention to my records. It wasn't enough to win consistently. I had to outdo—or at least match—the results I had in the past. When I failed, I would beat myself up. "I won twice as much money last May—what the hell is wrong with me?"

The answer was "probably nothing," but I had a hard time convincing myself of that. After all, the proof was in the records I kept.

So I decided to stop keeping records. I still know how much I've won and lost at the end of the year—I have to, for the tax man—but my days of keeping detailed session notes are behind me.

My own psyche aside, I still think it's absolutely necessary for a new player to keep those records. It's almost impossible to analyze your early results without them. But just be vigilant if those records start enabling a boatload of negative emotions to burrow their way into your brain, as mine did.

Remember, in the end it's all about the decisions. The results will take care of themselves.

The Inner Voice

If you read the e-mail from Sheets, you know he believes that poker players might have as many as 300 Factors to consider when making a decision.

As you play more and more poker, many of these considerations become automatic. Some of them become so deeply embedded in your consciousness that you may process them without ever being aware that you're doing so. The results sometimes manifest themselves as an "inner voice," letting you know, to paraphrase Kenny Rogers, when to hold'em or fold'em.

The process can be so unconscious that the inner voice might appear to be ESP, a nagging feeling, or even divine intervention. Whatever it is, learning to listen to it can be one of the best favors you can do for yourself as a poker player.

With 35 players left in the 2004 WSOP $1,500 no-limit Hold'em event, I was in trouble. Blinds were $800/$1,600, and I was down to about $10,000 in chips, looking for a spot to push all-in. Making matters worse, former WSOP champion Scotty Nguyen was at my table, raising with what seemed like every hand he was dealt. And winning. In a mere two hours, I had seen him single-handedly bust maybe eight players out of the tournament.

It seemed like business as usual when Scotty opened with a $4,400 raise. It seemed just as clear when I looked down to find A♥J♥, that I would push all-in.

Except I didn't. That inner voice told me to wait for a better spot. I listened. I folded. The big blind pushed all-in and Scotty called.

At first, it seemed as if the voice had led me astray. Scotty turned over A-10—a hand I had beat—and the big blind was making a move with K-9. I had had the best hand of the bunch and, if my raise had scared off the big blind, would have been a big favorite to double up against Scotty.

Scotty didn't need to improve, but he did, catching a 10 on the flop. A jack never came. Scotty knocked out another victim, and I breathed a huge sigh of relief, having dodged elimination.

You may be thinking that the voice gave me bad advice. After all, the numbers were on my side: I would have been a big favorite over Scotty, and even in a three-way pot I would have been getting more than enough equity to make a shot at tripling up worthwhile. I am convinced to this day, however, that my subconscious must have latched on to some other Factors. Maybe I noticed the big blind was itching to make a play. Maybe I remembered that I'd rather be the one making the initial raise than responding to a raiser. Maybe the poker gods were sending me a message.

I'll never know, but I'm glad I listened. Over the next four hands, I managed to double up, steal the blinds, and take down a decent pot with pocket kings, building my stack to $80,000. Oh, yeah: I wound up winning the tournament.

Trust your feelings. Even if they go against the numbers. Not every one of them will make obvious sense, but they are often "smarter" than you are.

The Wall

Not long ago, I spent a couple of weeks in Australia playing poker, splitting my time between cash games and tournaments. I returned home nearly $100,000 richer. But I was so depressed afterward that I holed up in a hotel room where I did nothing for four days and nights but sleep and watch TV.

Huh? Rewind that ... depressed? The trip was an enormous success, wasn't it?

Well, it was certainly a financial success. I finished second in a "speed" poker tournament and absolutely drilled a wild pot-limit Omaha game. I was riding a huge emotional high going into the $10,000 entry main event, and with 75 players left found myself with the third-biggest stack in the tournament. "Life is great!" I announced to myself.

I felt bold as I called a raise from a relatively tight opponent with A-3. I called his bet when the flop came Q-3-2, praying for another 3 to come on the turn. Prayer may have a lot of benefits outside of poker, but in my experience, when I'm praying at the table, it means I've put myself in a very, very bad spot. And then, miraculously, I thought my prayers had been answered when, in fact, the 3 did appear on the turn. I reraised him all-in ... and lost when he turned over pocket queens for a full house.

A few hands later, an opponent raised in front of me, betting all $80,000 or so of his chips hoping to win a $1,600 big blind. I squeezed my hand to find a queen and, once again, I found myself praying: "Please, let the second card be a queen so I can call him!"

And it was! And I did! And ... he had pocket aces. They held up to win him the hand.

Several hands later, everyone folded to the small blind, who paused after he looked at his cards. I knew from playing with him that his pause almost certainly meant he had a big hand. "No way I'm playing this hand," I said to myself. Sure enough, he raised, and sure enough, I called with a suited 8-6.

The flop came 9-6-2, and my opponent made a big bet. "He has a big hand," I thought as I pushed all of my chips into the middle. "I sure hope it's ace-king!"

Uh, no. He called, turning over pocket 10s. No miracle card arrived to save me.

In just three hands, I went from the top of the world to elimination. Even though I left Australia a substantial winner, I realized that I was not on top of my game. I was indecisive. I was ignoring my reads. I was *praying*. I had hit the wall. I realized it was just a matter of time before my results began to match my emotional state.

Poker players lie to one another for a living. The one person you can never lie to, though, is yourself. You need to be brutally honest about your emotions and whether they are affecting your game. The time to realize you are riding a roller coaster is *before* you start losing. Remember, you can lose just as much money on an emotional high as you can in the depths of despair.

Study your emotions with as much diligence as you would apply to any other aspect of the game. If you can learn how you will react to the hurdles and obstacles that are thrown in your path, you can start to forecast your emotional downswings and take an appropriate course of action. Great poker gets played when your mind is on an even keel, open to information and opportunities, seeing things clearly, and remembering them later.

Don't let taking a break from the game become a real-money decision. It's a lot harder to build a bankroll than it is to lose it. When you hit the wall, take some time away from the game—a week, a month, six months, whatever you need.

I emerged from my post-Australia four-day sleep-and-TV sabbatical with a refreshed mind and proceeded to have the best week of poker I'd experienced in six months.

> **Emotions—good or bad—can affect your play. Pay close attention to them.**

Keeping It Fun

Poker, especially when it's played well, can turn into a monotonous routine. Even I get bored playing like the Robot. When you're playing for a living, however, you can't afford to be bored. You don't get paid vacations or sick days.

I used to play $200 Sit-N-Gos all day with incredible results, often in the neighborhood of $300 an hour. The hardest part wasn't making money, but staying motivated enough to focus on the four or five tournaments I was participating in at any given moment.

It's no coincidence that most brick-and-mortar casinos position their poker rooms next to the sports books. Most people become poker players because they like to gamble, and when poker becomes a routine, they look for other ways to get their gamble on.

It didn't take long for my friends and me to discover *last-longer bets*. The concept was incredibly simple: Whoever lasted longer in the tournament won the bet. You'd be amazed at how much more interesting a $50 tournament becomes when you've got a $500 last-longer bet going with a friend or two.

But there was a hitch to our plan: Last-longer bets were fun, but they led us to make suboptimal tournament decisions. If one of us doubled up on a big hand, it put all kinds of pressure on the rest to double up as quickly as possible. Someone hanging on by a thread usually inspired the others to shut down, avoiding any kind of risk until the player in jeopardy had been eliminated. I once found myself folding pocket aces because one of the players I had bet with was down to his last two or three big blinds. "This can't be good," I remember thinking. Fun, but not good poker.

So we developed a new way to structure our last-longer bets, one that rewarded solid poker. In order to be eligible to win the entire amount of the last-longer bet, the winner also had to succeed in the tournament itself.

The winner's final finish in a ...		Percentage of the last-longer bet the winner is eligible to receive
... multi-table tournament	... single-table Sit-N-Go	
Top 10 percent	1st Place	100 percent
Top 20 percent	2nd Place	75 percent
Top 30 percent	3rd Place	50 percent
Worse than top 30 percent	4th Place or lower	25 percent
Bonuses		
Bounty for personally busting your opponent ...		+100 percent
Making the final table of a multi-table tournament ...		+50 percent

Let's say you make a $1,000 last-longer bet in a big multi-table tournament. Simply outlasting your opponent nets you only 25 percent of the bet, or $250. Last into the top 10 percent and make the final table, and you win 150 percent, or $1,500. And if you manage to knock out your opponent along the way, you stand to win $2,500!

Not only were these bets fun, they also encouraged us to play better poker—sometimes even with unintended benefits. After making a few of these bets, I realized there were strategies I could use to screw my last-longer opponents. First of all, I soon realized that if I was at the same table as an opponent, I wanted to be sitting as far away as possible—sitting too close tended to give one of us a significant positional advantage over the other. It took a little longer for me to figure out that when my opponent's stack dwindled to a point where he was in "push" mode—all-in or fold—I could use our distance to my advantage. Whenever he was in late position—an obvious spot for attacking the blinds—I would limp in from early position. This was usually enough to discourage him from moving all-in with anything but a great hand, leading him to pass up otherwise valuable opportunities to replenish his diminishing stack. Ha! The amazing thing was that my *other* opponents—the ones who weren't involved in the last-longer bet—usually interpreted my limping in from early position as a sign that I had a strong hand. So in addition to putting a wrench in my last-longer opponent's prospects, I won a few pots that I otherwise never would have played!

Last-longer bets aren't the only way to spice up a game. "Cross-booking" assigns a larger value to the chips that are in play, a difference that gets settled up after the game. For example, you and a friend might decide to each buy into a $1/$2 hold'em game for $100, but play for a 100x cross-book. If your opponent winds up with $15 more than you at the end of the session, you have to pay him 100 times the difference, or $1,500!

You can make all kinds of other proposition bets, like who will have the bigger stack at each tournament break. The best proposition bets force you to pay extra attention to the game. I love to take action on specific flops, like all spades or 2-4-6. Whenever that particular flop appears—and you notice it—your opponent has to pay you whatever you've decided to bet.

The point, of course, is to not let the monotony of playing poker every day affect your motivation to earn money. Side action is a good diversion and can improve your overall results as well!

Transitioning to Live Play

You can make a lot of money playing online poker, but the biggest scores, at least for now, come from playing live.

During my days as a dealer, I felt like I developed a good feel for the live game. Then I immersed myself in online poker. When I finally returned to a brick-and-mortar casino armed with my Factors approach to the game, I was brimming with confidence, certain I knew what to do with my cards in any given situation. I quickly discovered that playing poker in a live setting forced me to reconsider a few Factors that didn't exist in online play:

THE GAME IS SLOWER

Much slower. While that's often a good thing, giving you more time to think, it also gives you a lot more time to stew over your mistakes or the bad beats you've suffered. Or to get distracted by a nearby TV set or the really attractive person sitting at your table.

THERE ARE SOCIAL PRESSURES

Many gamblers treat their pastime as an isolating activity—after all, no one else can really feel the highs and lows they are experiencing with each bet won or lost. Online poker, while played against real opponents, doesn't do much to break the wall of isolation.

In a live setting, however, you can't scream "motherfucker!" at someone or punch the wall after a bad beat. You've got to control your emotions. You also have to deal with the emotions of every other person at the table.

EACH "HOUSE" HAS ITS OWN RULES

I remember sitting down to a game in London with a stack of bills in front of me, only to learn (at a critical and very expensive moment) that my cash "didn't play." Oops.

House rules aren't just limited to the way the game is played. The Bellagio, for example, doesn't have a snack bar near the poker room— tough for me, since I like to munch on junk food while I play. This may not seem like a big deal, until you sit down to a 3 p.m. tournament and discover you're not going to get a chance to eat until the dinner buffet at 9:30 p.m. Hunger can be a terrible distraction when no quick trip to the fridge is available.

Then there's the climate. Just about every casino I've played in has been too hot or too cold. I've been in tournaments where virtually everyone was on tilt because the air-conditioning was too powerful.

One of the greatest things about online poker is your ability to control your environment. When making the transition to live play, be aware that the environment can sometimes control you.

Chasing the Zone

My best results are the ones I don't remember.

Okay, that's not exactly true. What I mean to say is that my greatest successes at the poker table seem to come when I'm not consciously thinking about my results.

Athletes call it the Zone. Like Michael Jordan when he used to take over a game in the fourth quarter. Or Tiger Woods hitting balls with such precision that his opponents' games fall apart at the seams. Neither guy is thinking the ball into the hole. They are taking advantage of the countless hours of preparation that have led them to the present moment, giving them the luxury—and the incredible competitive advantage—of being able to shut their brains off.

Poker is the same way. The mathematics you use to make the "correct" play, the self-discipline that you need to avoid potentially dangerous situations, the practiced perception that will help you pick off an opponent's bluff at a key moment ... these will only take you so far. You will eventually discover that your best poker—and best results—come when you are playing by instinct, becoming one with the flow of the game the way a great surfer becomes inseparable from the wave he's riding.

No one is always in a perfect poker mind-set, especially me. Sometimes it seems like the harder I try to get there, the farther away I become. In the end, all any of us can do is to chase the Zone in the hopes of catching it, or maybe more accurately, having the Zone catch us.

I have tried, while writing this book, to share my strategies for chasing this elusive mind-set. Aggressiveness, routines, and positive superstitions are all a part of it. I hope that you will find them helpful, using them as a basis for forming your own strategies. With these techniques—and a lot of practice—anyone can become a poker champion.

I know this because I've been there. I'll be there again.

I look forward to seeing you there, too.

Hand Rankings

ROYAL FLUSH

A-K-Q-J-10, all of the same suit.

Ex.   A♣ K♣ Q♣ J♣ 10♣

STRAIGHT FLUSH

Any five consecutive cards of the same suit.

Ex.   2♦ 3♦ 4♦ 5♦ 6♦

FOUR OF A KIND

Four cards of the same rank.

Ex.   7♠ 7♦ 7♣ 7♥ 6♦

FULL HOUSE

Three cards of one rank, two of another.

Ex.   A♦ A♥ A♣ K♠ K♥

FLUSH

Any five cards of the same suit.

Ex.   A♥ J♥ 8♥ 7♥ 3♥

STRAIGHT

Five consecutive cards of any suit.

Ex.   Q♥ J♣ 10♣ 9♠ 8♦

THREE OF A KIND

Three cards of the same rank.

Ex.   4♠ 4♥ 4♦ 6♥ 3♣

TWO PAIR

Two pairs of different ranks.

Ex.   J♥ J♦ 5♥ 5♣ K♥

ONE PAIR

You guessed it:

Ex.   8♣ 8♠ 7♦ 6♥ A♣

HIGH CARDS

When no one has a hand, the high cards win. The ace is the highest card, then the king, etc.

Ex.   A♠ Q♦ 9♣ 4♦ 2♣   beats   A♦ J♣ 9♦ 4♣ 2♣

APPENDIX TWO:
The Rules

Texas Hold'em

When the old road gamblers from Texas brought this game to Las Vegas back in the 1960s, their reasoning was simple: They were the only ones who knew how to play. It was a perfect game to separate tourists from their money, as it offered a lot of low-risk, high-reward opportunities and presented good players with more information about what the bad ones might be playing than almost any other game.

Nowadays, you can't walk a city block without hearing somebody say: "I flopped a flush and pushed all-in, but he caught runner-runner 8s to make a full house on the river."

Everyone is playing Hold'em. The good news is, it's a relatively simple game to learn. Mastering it, however, is a whole different story.

Two hole cards are dealt to each player from a standard 52-card deck. In a casino game—where a professional dealer will normally be pitching the cards—a white button is used to mark the dealer's position, i.e., the player who would be dealing the cards if the players were actually dealing.

The two players to the left of the button are usually required to post blinds immediately before the deal: the small blind (just to the left of the button) must add a partial bet (usually half); the big blind (just to the left of the small blind) has to put in a full bet. The size of the bet is determined by the stakes at the table.

Action begins with the player seated just to the left of the big blind, who may decide to fold, call the minimum bet, or raise. In a limit Hold'em game, the raise will be a fixed amount, usually twice the minimum bet. The number of raises is usually capped, depending on the table rules, at three or four per round of betting.

The two blinds receive credit for the money they have already posted—if no one raises, the small blind has the option of completing the bet, while the big blind can check.

Once everyone has either folded or called whatever bets have been made, the dealer discards the top card (called the burn card) and deals three community cards—the flop—faceup on the table.

Action begins with the remaining player seated closest to the left of the button (the small blind, if he's still in the hand), with players checking, betting, raising, or folding in turn. Note that the button gets to act last on this (and every subsequent) round of betting.

Once the betting has been completed, the dealer burns another card and deals a fourth community card—called the turn card, or fourth street—faceup on the table. Once again, a round of action begins with the remaining player closest to the left of the button. In a limit game, the size of the bet usually doubles on fourth street.

After the action has been completed, the dealer burns one more card and deals the last community card—the river, or fifth street—faceup on the table. A final round of betting begins.

Once this round has ended, the remaining players turn over their hole cards, beginning with the player who made the last bet or raise (or, if no one has bet, the player closest to the left of the button).

The strength of each player's hand is determined by combining his two hole cards with the five community cards (also called the board) to make the best possible five-card hand. The best hand wins the pot.

In no-limit Hold'em, a player may bet as much money as he has in front of him at any time. If a player doesn't have enough money to call a bet, he may declare himself all-in, pushing in all of the chips he has left. Any portion of the current bet (and any later bets) that the all-in player cannot cover goes into a side pot. A player who pushes all-in is not eligible to win the side pot.

Pot-limit Hold'em is very similar to no-limit, except that a player cannot make a bet larger than the current size of the pot.

Omaha

Omaha is played identically to Texas Hold'em with one significant twist: Each player is dealt four hole cards instead of two and at the showdown must make a hand using two—and only two—of his hole cards in combination with only three community cards.

Players new to the game usually have a little trouble getting their head around this concept. There's little value, for example, in being dealt three or four of a kind, as you'll be able to use only two of them. Similarly, even if there are four or five suited cards on the board, you can't make a flush unless you have two cards of the same suit in your hand.

Omaha is often played hi-lo, eight-or-better. At the showdown, the pot is split between the players with the highest and lowest hands. A low hand must contain five unpaired cards, with no card higher than an 8, in order to qualify. Aces can be played as high or low cards, making A-2-3-4-5 the best possible low hand (there is no penalty for making a straight or flush with your low hand).

If there are no qualifying low hands, the player with the high hand *scoops* the pot, i.e., gets the whole enchilada. A player can also scoop the pot by making the best high hand *and* the best low hand. You can (and often will) use different combinations of hole and community cards to make your high and low hands.

Seven-Card Stud

There was a time, according to legend, before Texas Hold'em took over the world, when seven-card stud reigned supreme. Nowadays, it's becoming harder and harder to find a casino that deals stud poker, but it's still available in many online cardrooms.

Each player, after posting an ante, is dealt three cards: two face-down (the hole cards) and one face-up (the door card).

The player with the lowest door card is forced to make a mandatory partial bet, called the bring-in, its size dictated by the stakes at the table. If two (or more) players have the same low door card, the tie is broken by suit, ranked from lowest to highest as follows: clubs, diamonds, hearts, spades.

The player making the bring-in has the option of making a full bet. If he declines this option, play proceeds to the left, as each player may decide to fold, call the bring-in bet, or raise to a full bet.

Once everyone has folded or called the bet or raise(d), the dealer burns a card and deals each remaining player another faceup card, called fourth street. Action begins with the player whose upcards show the highest hand (with ties broken by suit—as above, spades are highest, clubs lowest) and continues in a clockwise direction around the table. Most games allow a player who has paired his upcards to bet twice the normal amount on fourth street.

After the action has been completed, the dealer burns another card and deals each remaining player a third up card, or fifth street. The action once again begins with the player who has the highest faceup hand. In most stud games, the amount that a player is allowed to bet doubles on fifth street.

Once the betting is done, the dealer again burns a card and deals a fourth and final faceup card, sixth street, to each remaining player. The player with the highest hand initiates the action. At the end of this round, the dealer burns the top card and deals each remaining player one last down card. The final round of betting begins with the player showing the highest hand. Once all bets and raises have been called, the hole cards are turned faceup, and the player whose seven cards make the highest five-card hand wins the pot.

It's possible for the dealer to run out of cards before the end of a hand. In most games, the dealer will gather all the discards, reshuffle them, and deal out the rest of the hand.

Seven-card stud is also often played hi-lo, eight-or-better. Low hands must qualify in the same way as they do in Omaha hi-lo (see the description above).

While you almost never find it played today, anyone who has ever seen *The Cincinnati Kid* knows that stud also comes in a five-card variety. The rules of five-card stud are essentially the same, except that each player is dealt two cards at the start—one down, one up—then three up cards, each followed by a round of betting.

Razz

You won't find this game spread too often on its own, but you've got to learn it if you're going to play H.O.R.S.E.—it's the "R"!

The rules are almost exactly the same as seven-card stud, except the object is to make the lowest possible hand. As a result, the bring-in must be made by the player showing the highest card, while the betting on subsequent rounds begins with the player whose up cards show the lowest hand. Aces are considered low cards, and flushes and straights don't count, so the best possible hand in Razz is A-2-3-4-5. Unlike eight-or-better games, hands don't have to qualify as low.

Deuce-to-Seven Triple Draw

While you won't find this game in many brick-and-mortar casinos, it is regularly spread in several online cardrooms and remains one of the more entertaining events at the World Series of Poker, where it's played with rebuys.

The goal is to make the lowest possible five-card hand. Unlike most other lowball games, straights and flushes do count against you, and aces are considered high cards. In other words, the best possible hand is an unsuited 2-3-4-5-7, or what players call "the Number Two." The next best hand—"the Number Three"—is an unsuited 2-3-4-6-7.

The betting structure is similar to Texas Hold'em: There is a button, and the two players to his left are required to post small and big blinds. Each player is dealt five down cards, and action begins with the player to the left of the big blind, who may fold, call, or raise.

Once the betting is done, each remaining player may stand pat with the hand he has, or discard anywhere from one to all five of his cards, drawing new (face down) cards to replace them. Another round of betting ensues, beginning with the player (closest) to the left of the button.

After everyone has acted, players may once again discard and draw up to five new cards. A new round of betting—usually at twice the limits of the previous round—begins with the remaining player closest to the left of the button.

The action is followed by a third draw and a final round of betting. The cards are turned face up, and the lowest hand wins.

This game is occasionally played Ace-to-Five. The rules are the same, except aces are low and players aren't penalized for making straights or flushes.

Badugi!

While you may not have heard of this game yet, you will soon! I love Badugi, as it combines poker psychology with a lot of action.

Badugi is similar to the triple-draw games described above, except that each player is dealt four cards instead of five and—here's the twist—you aren't allowed to play any card that makes a pair or is the same suit as another. The goal is to get a badugi—four unpaired cards, all of different suits. Aces are low, so the best possible badugi would be a hand like A♠ 2♣ 3♦ 4♥.

You won't make a badugi every time, as you'll usually have to eliminate one or two (or, very rarely, three) cards from your hand at the showdown because they are pairs or are the same suit as another card. A hand like A♠ 2♣ 3♦ 4♦ may look unbeatable, but you can't play the 4♦ because you already have the 3♦—you can show down only a three-card hand (A♠ 2♣ 3♦). With a hand like A♠ 2♣ 2♦ 3♠, you can only show a two-card hand—A♠ 2♣—as you aren't allowed to play the 2♦ (which pairs your 2♣) or the 3♠ (which is the same suit as your A♠). A four-card badugi always beats a three-card hand, a three-card hand beats a two-card hand, and a two-card hand beats a one-card hand.

The betting structure is the same as any other triple-draw game. Two players post blinds, then action begins with the under-the-gun player seated two to the left of the button. After a round of betting, each player—beginning with the closest to the left of the button—can discard and draw zero to four new cards. After a second round of betting, a second draw. In limit badugi, the size of the bet doubles on the third round of betting. A third and final draw, followed by a final round of betting. Showdown.

Odds and Outs

I don't think you have to be great at math to play poker. Sure, it would be great to know the exact odds surrounding any situation you happen to find yourself in, but intuition and common sense can make up for more than enough percentage points if all you have is a rough idea.

How do you get a rough idea? It starts with an understanding of how a poker player makes money. It's not just enough to win pots. Winning more pots than everyone else doesn't guarantee that you're going to make the most money. Or even wind up ahead.

Winning players know that every pot is an investment opportunity; you risk some money in the hopes of winning more than you've risked. By making good decisions—"positive equity" decisions—over the long term, your investments will show a positive return.

Pot Odds

Before you can determine your equity in any situation, you have to start by determining whether or not an opportunity *might* be profitable.

Poker players use *pot odds* to judge potential profitability. Let's say, for example, there is $90 in the pot, and you have to call a $10 bet to stay in the hand. The pot is said to be "laying" you odds of 90-to-10, or 9-to-1. You have to spend $10 to have a chance of winning it, but you will get $100 (the $90 plus the $10 you added) when you do.

In order to break even in this situation, you have to win the pot one out of every 10 times you decide to call the bet. You can lose nine straight times (spending $90), but as long as you win the 10th (risking $10 but taking in $100), you'll cover whatever you've spent. For this to be a positive equity situation, your odds of winning the pot have to be better than 1 in 10, or 10 percent.

Outs

The trickiest part of the whole process is figuring out just how often you will win the pot.

One of the main reasons Texas Hold'em became such a popular game among professionals is the huge amount of information available once you see the flop. With three rounds of betting to go, you're less than halfway through the hand, but you already know five of the seven cards that you'll have to make your hand. You are also able to put your opponents on a range of hands—after all, you can see 60 percent of their cards—and figure out which cards, on the turn and the river, will improve your hand into one that's likely to win.

The cards that can help you are called outs. Sometimes you will have a lot ...

YOU: A♥ K♥   THE FLOP: J♥ 10♥ 2♣

All you have currently is ace high, but any heart—there are nine left unaccounted for—will make you a nut flush, any of the three queens (you've already counted the Q♥) makes a nut straight, and an ace or a king (three of each, making six) gives you top pair. Add them up, and you have 18 cards that could improve your hand.

Sometimes you have very few outs ...

YOU: 2♥ 2♣   THE FLOP: A♦ 10♦ 4♦

The only way your pair of 2s can get better is to catch a third deuce. But notice that if the 2♦ comes up, it will make a flush for anyone holding a diamond, so it's probably not the card you want to see. Your only "clean" out is the 2♠—assuming someone hasn't already flopped a flush.

In order to figure out the chances of catching an out on the turn or the river, you can add a bunch of fractions ... or you can use a method poker pro Phil Gordon calls "the rule of four and two"—you can estimate the percentage of catching an out …

> … with two cards to come (the turn and river), by multiplying the number of outs by four;

> … with one card to come (the river), by multiplying the number of outs by two.

In the first example, where you had 18 outs, your chances of landing one on the turn or river are 18 x 4, or about 72 percent. Pretty good odds! Miss the turn, and those odds drop to 18 x 2 = 36 percent.

Comparing those odds to the size of the pot will give you an idea of the equity you are getting on your call. With a 36 percent chance of catching a card on the river, for example, you'll wind up winning about once every three times. As long as the pot is laying you somewhere in the neighborhood of 2-to-1 odds, you are good to call!

Why None of This Is Extremely Important

A lot of poker books spend a lot of time talking about percentages and pot odds. Since you had to make it all the way to the appendices to read this, you're right in guessing that this is not one of those books.

It's not that I don't think odds are important—it's pretty obvious that you should preserve your chips for situations when you have positive equity. But there are a couple of reasons why I think odds are less important than people make them out to be.

THE POSITIVE EQUITY DECISION IS NOT ALWAYS THE BEST DECISION

Let's say I'm confronted with a decision to call a bet with a hand that has a 1-in-8 chance of winning. The pot is laying me odds of 20-to-1. In a never-ending cash game with an unlimited bankroll, this is an easy call. In a tournament, however, where that call might put me all-in, I'll often have to fold—my chips are too precious. When you can't replenish your bankroll, short-term survival becomes more important than long-term positive equity.

ODDS ARE NEARLY IMPOSSIBLE TO CALCULATE ACCURATELY

In the example above, I used a really simple situation: calling $10 to win $100. In real life, it's rarely that clear-cut. What happens if you miss the turn and have to call a $20 bet to see the river? How many players are likely to keep calling bets (or making raises) throughout the rest of the hand? How much bigger will the pot be? Do you have a chance of leading an opponent to make a mistake that will cost him his entire stack? What if the turn card changes the texture of the board, increasing or reducing the number of outs that you have? It's hard enough accounting for these variables in a Hold'em game—try it in Omaha, where the four cards you're holding make it almost certain that every new card on the board will create lots of new possibilities.

Implied odds—the "true" odds you'll be getting on your decision when all of the money is in the pot—can give you the justification to take all kinds of crazy risks when the odds are seemingly against you. I'm in a no-limit tournament with $1,000 in chips, and an opponent makes a $20 bet into me. If I suspect that I can win his entire stack should I hit my card—and he's got a big enough stack to make it worthwhile—then I may be willing to take chances with hands that the current pot odds would have demanded I throw away.

THERE ARE DIFFERENT KINDS OF EQUITY

One incredibly important Factor in any decision is fold equity: the increase in equity that comes with the chance a bet from you will lead an opponent to fold without a showdown. But how do you determine fold equity? Can you really say that a person has a 30 percent chance of folding? Are you sure it's not 20 percent or 40 percent? You are, at best, making a best guess.

There are other kinds of equity as well. In the late stages of tournaments, players with very big stacks will sometimes call players with very small stacks even if the odds don't warrant it, because the upside of eliminating an opponent and moving up the prize ladder outweighs the relatively small dent their stack will take should they lose. There are players who will call bets they "shouldn't" as part of a table image they'll exploit later, or to drive a tilting opponent over the edge into insanity with a bad beat.

Let me sum it up this way: While there may be a correct answer to "What do the odds say I should do?" in every situation, to figure it out you would have to be an omnipotent poker god, with a supercomputer for a brain, who knows exactly how each card and action would affect the decision-making process of every player involved in a hand.

We mere mortals rely on a basic understanding of the odds … and a lot of guesswork. The more you play, the better a feel you'll develop for the game, and the better your guesses will become.

Tournament Structures

Here's a sample tournament structure for a Sit-N-Go. Each player begins with $1,000 in chips, and each level lasts 10 hands …

Level	Small Blind	Big Blind	Ante
1	7	15	0
2	15	30	0
3	25	50	0
4	50	100	0
5	100	200	0
6	200	400	0
7	300	600	0
8	500	1000	0

Here's a sample tournament structure for a multi-table tournament. Each player begins with $1,500 in chips, and each level lasts 10 minutes ...

Level	Small Blind	Big Blind	Ante
1	7	15	0
2	15	30	0
3	25	50	0
4	50	100	0
5	100	200	0
6	200	400	0
7	300	600	0
5-minute break			
8	150	300	25
9	200	400	50
10	300	600	75
11	400	800	100
12	600	1200	150
13	800	1600	200
5-minute break			
14	1200	2400	300
15	1500	3000	400
16	2000	4000	500
17	3000	6000	750
18	4000	8000	1000
19	6000	12000	1500
5-minute break			
20	8000	16000	2000
21	12000	24000	3000
22	15000	30000	4000
23	20000	40000	5000
24	30000	60000	6000
25	40000	80000	8000
5-minute break			
26	60000	120000	10000
27	100000	200000	10000

Glossary

add-on	A feature of some tournaments that allows players to purchase additional tournament chips with real-world cash.
aggressive	Tending to bet and raise (as opposed to check and call). The opposite of *passive*.
all-in	The state or act of risking all of one's remaining chips on the outcome of a hand.
ante	Per the rules of some games, a mandatory bet before the start of a hand.
ATM	As in the cash machine: a bad player who generates cash for his opponents.
backdoor	To complete a flush or straight with two running cards.
bad beat	A statistically improbable loss, usually accompanied by uncontrollable feelings of rage and the desire to share the circumstances with anyone who will listen (willingly or otherwise).
bad-beat story	The story of incredible misfortune that accompanies a bad beat. Usually not interesting to anyone except the person telling it.
badugi	A form of draw poker in which players try to make hands that are low and contain cards of different suits.
big bet	The amount in a limit poker game that players are required to bet and raise during the later stages of a hand.
big blind	A mandatory bet, usually posted before the deal by the player two seats to the left of the dealer, designed to help create a pot worth contesting.

207

Big Slick	In Texas Hold'em, the nickname for A-K, one of the strongest and most frustrating hands to play.
blind	A mandatory bet that certain players (based on their seat) are required to post before the cards are dealt.
blind structure	In a poker tournament, the rules that govern the scheduled increases in blinds and antes, more or less controlling the length of the tournament.
board	In many poker games, the face up community cards that players may combine with their own hole cards to make a hand.
board texture	The range of possible hands that the board might allow.
boat	A full house.
bottom pair	A pair made with the lowest card on the board.
bubble	In a tournament, the period of time that separates the players who are close to making the money from those who actually make the money.
button	Usually depicted as a white disc that moves clockwise around the table with each hand, the button represents the "dealer" position, considered the most advantageous in many games because it is the last to act on most rounds of betting.
buy-in	The entry fee to a tournament, or the amount of chips a player chooses to begin with in a cash game.
calling station	A loose, passive poker player. See also *ATM*.
cap	The limit many casinos put on the number of bets that can be made in any single round of a limit poker game.
cash machine	See *ATM*.
connectors	Closely grouped cards that can be used to make a straight.
continuation bet	A follow-up bet made by a player who has previously represented a very strong hand, aimed at reminding everyone that he is representing a strong hand.
counterfeit	When a card screws up a hand that you have already made. For example, if you are holding A-4 in a Hold'em game and the flop comes A-5-4, a 5 on the turn or river will counterfeit your pair of fours.
crippled	Used to describe the deck when you or an opponent is holding one or more cards that other players might need to improve their hands—for example, when you are holding A-K and the flop comes A-K-K.

crying call	The act of calling a bet out of frustration in a situation where you are sure you are probably beat. Often part of a bad beat story.
cutoff	The seat just to the right of the button.
dead money	The players in a cash game or tournament who have little or no chance of winning and exist therefore to pad the wallets of the better players.
dealer	The person who deals the cards and, in many games, has the advantage of being last to act during the betting. Since most online games don't require the players themselves to do any actual dealing, the dealer's position is usually represented by a button that moves clockwise around the table with each hand.
donkey	A terrible poker player.
door card	In stud games, the first up card (third street) dealt to each player.
double belly-buster	A hand that allows a player to complete a gut-shot straight draw with two different cards. For example, in Hold'em, a player holding Q-10 with a 9-8-6 flop can make a straight with a J or a 7.
double up	To double one's stack on a single hand, usually as the result of an all-in bet.
drawing dead	Having no chance of making a hand that will beat your opponent's. For example, having only a straight draw when someone else has already made a flush.
drawing hand	A hand that may not currently be the best hand but has a chance to improve should the right cards come.
expected value	The amount, based on the laws of long-term probability, that you should expect to earn or lose from a certain decision.
fifth street	In hold'em and Omaha, the fifth (and last) community card, also known as the *river*. In stud games, the third "up" card (and fifth overall card) dealt to each player.
field	The total number of entrants in a tournament.
fish	See donkey.
flop	In certain poker games, the first three community cards that are laid on the table.
fold equity	The extra value a bettor receives from the chance that his opponent might fold to his bet.
fourth street	In Hold'em and Omaha, the fourth community card, also known as the turn. In stud games, the second up card (and fourth overall card) dealt to each player

free card	A card that a player gets to see without having to call a bet, often the result of an aggressive play made at an earlier point in the hand.
gut-shot	A straight that can be filled only by a single card. For example, if you have 9-6 and the flop comes 10-8-5, only a 7 will make you a straight.
"hand of God"	A tournament strategy in which a strong player intentionally passes up an opportunity to eliminate a weaker one. See Chapter Four.
hand selection	The range of hands that a player is willing to play in any specific situation.
heads-up	A hand that has come down to just two players.
hidden pair	A pair consisting solely of down cards, thus totally concealed from the rest of the world.
hit-and-run artist	A vile form of poker player who looks to make a quick score—often via a *bad beat*—then leave the table before he has a chance to lose it.
Hole cards	The down cards dealt to each player.
H.O.R.S.E.	An event in which the game alternates with each orbit, among Hold'em, Omaha hi-lo, Razz, seven-card stud, and seven-card stud hi-lo eight-or-better.
implied pot odds	The odds surrounding a decision that are based not on the current amount of money in the pot but on the end result of all of the betting that will take place before the end of the hand.
junk	Cards that are unlikely to make a strong hand.
kicker	An unpaired high card in a player's hand that may, in certain situations, be used to determine the winner of the hand—the pot going to the player with the higher kicker.
leak	A small, consistent error that, over time, can add up to big losses. Can also be used to describe a non-poker expense that hurts your poker bankroll, like craps, drugs or strippers.
limp	To enter a pot without a raise.
loose	A tendency to play a lot of hands. The opposite of tight.
middle pair	A hand that pairs a hole card with a community card that's neither the highest nor the lowest on the board.
monster	A very, very strong hand.
muck	To throw one's hand into the discard pile without showing it. The term is also used to describe the discard pile itself.

multi-table tour-nament (MTT)	A tournament with enough entrants to require simultaneous action on more than one table.
no-limit	A game in which players are allowed to bet as much as they have in front of them (usually above a certain minimum) at any point in the hand.
nuts	The best possible hand that can be made given the nature of the board.
offsuit	Two hole cards of different suits.
on tilt	Being angry or frustrated at the poker table, which can lead you to make bad decisions.
open-ended	A straight draw that can be completed by a card on either end. For example, a Hold'em player with K-10 who gets a Q-J-3 flop can make a straight with either an A or a 9.
orbit	The period of time it takes for the button to make a complete revolution around the table.
out	An available card that will improve a hand.
overbet	A bet that seems too large for the circumstances..
overpair	A pocket pair that is higher than any card on the board.
passive	Tending to check and call (as opposed to bet and raise). The opposite of aggressive.
pigeon	See donkey, fish.
pocket pair	In hold'em, a hidden pair.
position	The location of one's seat relative to the dealer, used to determine the order in which each player must act.
pot-committed	Having invested so many of your chips in a pot that the odds pretty much demand you call any future bets.
pot odds	The amount required to call a bet compared with the amount already in the pot in relation to your odds of making the best hand.
pot-limit	A hybrid of limit and no-limit poker in which a player may bet any amount up to the current size of the pot.
premium hands	The best starting hands, more likely to win than any other.
prize structure	In a tournament, the rules governing the distribution of prize money, i.e., the number of players paid and the amount each receives.
prop	A player hired by a cardroom to sustain certain games at specific times of day.

rags	Cards that are unlikely to have helped anyone. For example, in Hold'em, a flop such as A-6-2 might be described as "Ace-rag-rag."
rainbow	A flop or board featuring cards of different suits, which make a flush very unlikely or altogether impossible.
rake	The amount the house takes out of each pot in exchange for hosting the game.
rebuy	A feature of some tournaments that allows players who have lost all their chips (or fallen below a certain level) to buy more tournament chips with real-world cash.
river	In Hold'em and Omaha, the last community card (also known as fifth street).
rock	A tight player who usually doesn't enter a pot without a premium hand and, when he does enter a pot, is unlikely to make or call a bet unless he has a very strong hand.
satellite	A tournament whose winner or winners earn spots in another tournament with a bigger buy-in.
scare card	A card that looks like it might complete one (or more) very strong hands.
scoop	In hi-lo games, to take the entire pot, either because the hand wins the high and the low, or because no hand is low enough to be eligible to win.
semi-bluff	A bet made with a hand that, while not currently the strongest, has a chance to improve.
set	Three of a kind, made from a pocket pair and a card on the board.
shorthanded	A game with a smaller-than-usual number of players.
Sit-N-Go	A tournament, often at a single table, that begins when enough players have signed up to fill the seats.
small bet	The amount in a limit poker game that players are required to bet and raise during the early stages of a hand.
small blind	A mandatory partial bet, usually posted before the deal by the player just to the left of the dealer.
smooth call	To call with a hand that you intend to raise with on a later street.
split pair	In stud games, a pair made up of a door card and a hole card.
stack	The total number of chips possessed by a player.

stand pat	In a draw poker game, to pass up the opportunity to select new cards.
stealing the blind	The act of making a raise, usually in late position, in the hopes of winning the blinds without a contest.
stuck	In the negative column.
suckout	A statistically improbable victory against a hand that is favored to win.
suited	Two hole cards of the same suit, which improve the chances of making a flush.
suited connector	Cards that are both suited and connectors, improving the chances of making a straight or a flush.
super-satellite	A multi-table satellite tournament.
table image	The "personality" you have exhibited at the table to the extent that it affects the way your opponents choose to play against you.
tell	An unconscious action that may tip off your opponents to the true nature of your hand.
tight	Likely to enter pots with very few hands. The opposite of loose.
top pair	A pair made with a hole card and the highest card on the board.
trips	Three of a kind.
turn	In Hold'em or Omaha, the fourth community card (also known as fourth street).
under the gun	The player, usually seated just to the left of the *big blind*, who has to make the first decision at the start of a hand.
underbet	A bet that seems to be too small given the circumstances.
value bet	A bet made at the end of a hand that should, in the long term, show positive results, regardless of the outcome of that particular hand.

Session Notes

Date	In	Out	Time	Bankroll	Stakes	Starting Chips	Ending Chips	Results	Notes

Date	In	Out	Time	Bankroll	Stakes	Starting Chips	Ending Chips	Results	Notes

Date	In	Out	Time	Bankroll	Stakes	Starting Chips	Ending Chips	Results	Notes

Date	In	Out	Time	Bankroll	Stakes	Starting Chips	Ending Chips	Results	Notes

Date	In	Out	Time	Bankroll	Stakes	Starting Chips	Ending Chips	Results	Notes

Date	In	Out	Time	Bankroll	Stakes	Starting Chips	Ending Chips	Results	Notes

Date	In	Out	Time	Bankroll	Stakes	Starting Chips	Ending Chips	Results	Notes

Date	In	Out	Time	Bankroll	Stakes	Starting Chips	Ending Chips	Results	Notes

Date	In	Out	Time	Bankroll	Stakes	Starting Chips	Ending Chips	Results	Notes

Acknowledgments

LET ME START BY saying thanks to Jonathan Grotenstein, for not only helping me to put my thoughts on paper but making me sound halfway coherent in the process.

I'm not the most organized human being on this planet, a fact my sister, Beth, helps me to conceal pretty much on an hourly basis. She and the rest of my family have always been incredibly supportive, regardless of the challenges I've thrown their way. I love all of you very much.

Without my friend Jordan Salmon, I never would have started playing this damn game. And without friends like the Crew and Darrell "Gigabet" Dicken, I probably wouldn't have become any good at it. Thanks to everyone who has helped me to expand my mental capacity for cards, life, and everything in between.

Millions of thanks—literally—to Eric "Sheets" Haber and Mark Dickstein, who, for lack of a better word, "invented" my poker career when they decided to take a chance on a group of kids with a lot more ambition than cash. I will always be grateful to the two of you for recognizing our talent and potential and giving us the opportunity to be successful. Double thanks to Sheets for also introducing me to Cliff "Johnny Bax" Josephy—I can't tell you how much I appreciate the two of you for always being there for me.

Thanks to everyone who contributed to this book, including the already mentioned Gigabet, Sheets, and Johnny Bax, as well as Phil Hellmuth Jr., Mark Seif, Thomas "Thunder" Keller, Michael "The Grinder" Mizrachi, Carlos Mortensen, and Noah "Exclusive" Boeken.

Finally, I'd like to thank all the people who made this book come together—Greg Dinkin and Frank Scatoni of Venture Literary, plus Michael Solomon, Jaime Lowe, Adrienne Onofri, and the rest of the team at ESPN Books. You guys took a chance on a first-time author who barely survived a year of college.

—Scott Fischman